Workbook

Housing and Interior Design

11th Edition

Claudia D. Lazok
Tucson, Arizona

Evelyn L. Lewis
Professor Emerita, Home Economics
Northern Arizona University
Flagstaff, Arizona

Textbook by
Evelyn L. Lewis and Carolyn Turner Smith

D1709865

Publisher
Goodheart-Willcox Company, Inc.
Tinley Park, IL
www.g-w.com

Contents

Unit 1
Housing—Human Factors and Influences

Unit 2
The Built Environment and Space Planning

Unit 3
Fundamentals of Interior Design

Unit 4
The Process of Interior Design

Unit 5
Interior Surfaces, Materials, and Furnishings

Chapter 27

Preparing for Career Success

Chapter 28

Entrepreneurship for Housing and Interiors

Chapter 1

The Human Need for Housing

Human Needs

Activity A   Name_____

Chapter 1   Date_____   Period _____

Complete the pyramid of Maslow's hierarchy of human needs. Explain each need and describe ways in which housing can help to fulfill it.

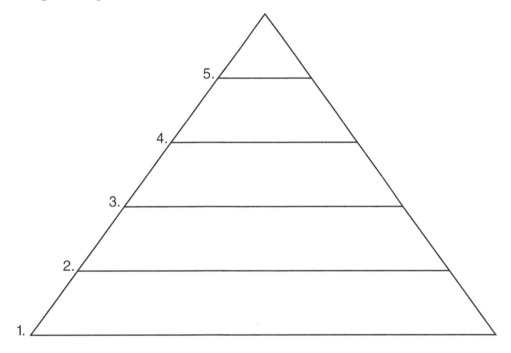

1. Need: _____   Explanation: _____

    Ways in which housing can fulfill this need: _____

2. Need: _____   Explanation: _____

    Ways in which housing can fulfill this need: _____

3. Need: _____   Explanation: _____

    Ways in which housing can fulfill this need: _____

4. Need: _____   Explanation: _____

    Ways in which housing can fulfill this need: _____

5. Need: _____   Explanation: _____

    Ways in which housing can fulfill this need: _____

Your Housing Needs and Values

Activity B   Name_____

Chapter 1   Date_____   Period _____

In the space that follows, place a *website link* (URL) of a room photo that reflects your needs and values, attach a photo of a room that reflects your needs and values, or draw your ideal room. List three needs addressed by the room image and indicate if each is physical or psychological in nature. Identify a value associated with each need.

Need	Value

Space and Privacy Needs

Activity C   Name_____

Chapter 1   Date_____   Period_____

Working with three or four classmates, compare factors that affect people's space and privacy needs. Each team member should use the interview questions below to interview a person. (No more than one person should be interviewed in each of the age categories listed.) Report your findings to the team and answer the discussion questions that follow.

Interview Questions

1. Which category includes your age?

   _____5–10 _____11–16 _____17–21 _____22–30 _____31–45 _____46–60 _____ over 60

2. How many people live in your home? _____

3. What is the smallest size home in which you would feel comfortable?_____

4. Why?_____

5. What rooms, areas, or objects in your home do you consider part of your private space?

   _____

   _____

6. Why?_____

   _____

7. How do you spend time in your private space?_____

   _____

8. What problems have you had in keeping your private space to yourself?_____

   _____

   _____

Discussion Questions

1. How does age affect people's space and privacy needs? _____

   _____

   _____

2. How do hobbies and activities affect people's space and privacy needs? _____

   _____

   _____

3. How does the value of family unity affect people's space needs? _____

   _____

   _____

Lifestyles

Name_____

Date_____ Period _____

Examine the images of two different houses for sale that reflect different lifestyles. In the space provided, identify and describe the lifestyle each image represents. List your opinion of the advantages and disadvantages of each type of home.

Image 1

rSnapshotPhotos/Shutterstock.com

Lifestyle: _____

Description:_____

_____

_____

_____

Advantages: _____

_____

_____

_____

Disadvantages:_____

_____

_____

_____

Image 2

Lifestyle: _____

Description:_____

_____

_____

_____

Advantages: _____

_____

_____

_____

Disadvantages:_____

_____

_____

_____

Jeramey Lende/Shutterstock.com

Family Stages

Name_____

Date_____ Period _____

Conduct an interview of one or two members of a family to learn about its housing needs. Then answer the questions that follow.

1. What are the ages of the family members living at home as well as away from home?_____

_____

_____

2. In what stage of the family life cycle is this family? Explain. _____

_____

_____

3. In what substage(s) of the family life cycle is this family? _____

_____

Explain. _____

_____

_____

_____

_____

4. What are the present housing needs of this family? _____

_____

_____

_____

_____

_____

_____

5. How might the housing needs of this family change in the future? _____

_____

_____

_____

_____

_____

_____

_____

Green Choices for the Environment

Name_____

Date_____ Period _____

In the space provided, identify green and sustainable design choices that can help solve current environmental problems. Then describe how solving these problems will improve housing and the quality of life for society. Use Internet resources for research as needed.

1. Noise pollution: _____

_____

_____

_____

_____

2. Air pollution: _____

_____

_____

_____

_____

3. Traffic congestion:_____

_____

_____

_____

_____

4. Waste of natural resources: _____

_____

_____

_____

_____

5. How will solving these problems improve housing and the quality of life for society?

_____

_____

_____

_____

_____

_____

Factors Influencing Housing

Relating Historical Events to Housing

Activity A   Name_____

Chapter 2   Date _____   Period _____

Use your text and online or print sources to research housing during one of the following periods: 1700s, 1800s, or 1900s. In the following chart, describe the type of housing used and summarize the historical events that influenced housing during this period. Then describe changes that are taking place in housing and the housing industry today.

Housing period: _____

Type of Housing Used	Historical Influences

Changes in housing today: _____

_____

_____

_____

Cultural and Societal Influences on Housing

Activity B   Name _____

Chapter 2   Date _____   Period _____

Part 1: Describe current cultural influences on housing and the effects of cultural influences from previous eras on housing today. Record your responses on additional paper and attach to this worksheet, if necessary.

Current cultural influences: _____

_____

_____

_____

_____

Cultural influences from previous eras: _____

_____

_____

_____

_____

Part 2: Visit the U.S. Census Bureau website to locate information about population increases, types of housing, household size, and household composition in the United States over the past 20 years. Record your findings in the following chart. Then describe the effects that societal trends in marriage and divorce rates, family size, and life expectancy have on housing today.

	Current	**5 Years Ago**	**10 Years Ago**	**15 Years Ago**	**20 Years Ago**
Population Increase					
Types of Housing					
Household Size					
Household Composition					

Effects of societal trends on housing: _____

_____

_____

_____

_____

Housing Environments

Activity C

Chapter 2

Name_____

Date_____   Period _____

Complete the following exercises on housing environments.

Part 1: For these ten items below, place one letter in each blank as follows: *N* if the term describes the natural environment; *C* if the term describes the constructed environment; and *B* if the term describes the behavioral environment.

_____ 1. intelligence

_____ 2. land

_____ 3. house

_____ 4. climate

_____ 5. solar energy

_____ 6. talent

_____ 7. landscape

_____ 8. air conditioner

_____ 9. happiness

_____ 10. water

Part 2: Use online or print sources to find an article or picture of each of the following environments. Insert the website link or URL of each picture in the space provided or attach a copy of the picture. Using descriptive words, explain how each of these articles or pictures relates to the housing environment.

URL for natural environment:_____

Ways in which this relates to the housing environment: _____

_____

_____

_____

_____

_____

_____

_____

_____

_____

_____

(Continued)

URL for constructed environment: _____

Ways in which this relates to the housing environment: _____

_____

_____

_____

_____

_____

URL for behavioral environment: _____

Ways in which this relates to the housing environment: _____

_____

_____

_____

_____

_____

Give an example of how one type of environment can overlap another type: _____

_____

_____

_____

_____

_____

_____

_____

Housing and the Economy

Name_____

Date_____ Period _____

Use online or print sources to compare the effects of the economy on housing in the periods shown in the following chart. Describe government response to each crisis. Then identify ways to prevent the impact of economic recession on housing in the future.

	The Great Depression (beginning 1929)	Financial Crisis (beginning 2007)
Gross Domestic Product (GDP)		
Population		
Housing Prices		
Housing Starts		
Unemployment Rate		
Homeless Rate		

Government response: _____

_____

_____

_____

_____

Ways to prevent the impact of economic recession on housing: _____

_____

_____

_____

_____

_____

Housing Legislation

Name_____

Date_____ Period _____

In the space provided, describe ways in which federal, state, or local housing legislation helps people face the following circumstances. Then identify at least one piece of legislation from text *Figure 2.25* for each circumstance.

Age discrimination: _____

_____

_____

_____

Racial discrimination: _____

_____

_____

_____

Low income: _____

_____

_____

_____

Natural catastrophes: _____

_____

_____

_____

Physical disabilities: _____

_____

_____

_____

Homelessness: _____

_____

_____

_____

Chapter 3

Decision Making and Housing Options

Thought Involved in Making Decisions

Activity A   Name_____

Chapter 3   Date_____   Period _____

Imagine that you are an interior designer. Complete the following exercises on decisions.

Case 1—Decorating Design Decisions

1. The color and style of the draperies in your client's living room need to be changed to coordinate with new furnishings recently purchased. You present your client with the exact color and style of draperies. You discuss the choice with your client. What type of decision have you and your client made?

   _____

2. While looking for a wall covering design to match the fabric swatches for one client's bedroom, you see a pattern that could be used in the bathroom of another client. You purchase the wall covering needed for the bathroom, but have not thought about how it will look or even if it is what your client will want. What type of decision have you made?

   _____

3. In which decision were the consequences considered? _____

   _____

4. In which decision was little thought given to possible outcomes?_____

   _____

5. What are some possible negative outcomes of each decision?_____

   _____

6. Which decision is likely to give your clients more long-term satisfaction? _____

   _____

Case 2—Routine Decisions

7. Your phone rings on a weekday morning. You answer the phone. A client wants to make an appointment with you. You make some notes regarding the conversation and add the appointment to your schedule. What type of decision have you made?

   _____

8. What are some possible advantages of this type of decision? _____

   _____

9. What are some possible disadvantages of this type of decision? _____

   _____

10. What events could occur when you check your appointment schedule that would change the type of decision made?

   _____

Decision Groupings

Name_____

Date_____   Period_____

Read the following paragraph. In the chart below, list a possible central-satellite decision and a possible chain decision based on the information provided. (You may make your own assumptions about any information that is not provided. Both decisions may be based on the same or different assumptions.) Then, for the central-satellite decision, list at least five related but independent decisions. For the chain decision, list at least five decisions triggered by the original decision that must be made to complete the action. *Optional:* After listing the decisions in each column below, create a diagram for each decision on a separate sheet of paper and attach it to this activity.

> The Benson family always uses the municipal pool in town for swimming in the summer, but the city has decided to close the pool. The Bensons do not want to stop summertime swimming, so they must decide on an alternative. They have many options. They could join a private pool in the area for about three times the cost of the city municipal pool. They could use the municipal pool in the next city at a slightly higher cost, but more time would be spent traveling to and from the pool. The Bensons could buy a pool for their backyard. The initial cost could be very high depending on the type of pool purchased. Money, however, would be saved in pool memberships, and the pool would be very convenient.

The Bensons might decide on the following central-satellite decisions and chain decisions:

Central-satellite Decision	Chain Decision
_____	_____
_____	_____
Related, but independent decisions:	**Other decisions to make to complete the action:**
_____	_____
_____	_____
_____	_____
_____	_____
_____	_____
_____	_____

How would you compare using the central-satellite decision process to the chain decision process in making this decision?

_____

_____

_____

_____

Resources

Name_____

Date_____   Period _____

List your human, nonhuman, and community resources in order of importance to you. Then describe why these resources are important.

1. List five of your own human resources in order of importance to you.

_____

_____

_____

_____

_____

Why do you consider these human resources important? _____

_____

_____

2. List five of your own nonhuman resources in order of importance to you.

_____

_____

_____

_____

_____

Why do you consider these nonhuman resources important?_____

_____

_____

3. List five of your own community resources in order of importance to you.

_____

_____

_____

_____

_____

Why do you consider these community resources important? _____

_____

_____

Human Resources

Name_____

Date_____ Period _____

Assume you are an interior designer working with two client families. For the purpose of this activity, assess the human resources of two families you know, imagining they are your clients. Rate each family member on a scale of 0 (poor) to 10 (good) in the chart that follows. Then analyze their ratings by answering the questions and the directions that follow on the next page.

Inventory of Human Resources					
Human Resources	**Physical Health**	**Energy Level**	**Knowledge Level**	**Abilities/ Skills**	**Attitude**
Client Family 1					
Husband/Father:					
Wife/Mother:					
Teens:					
Children:					
Others:					
Total Members:					
Client Family 2					
Husband/Father:					
Wife/Mother:					
Teens:					
Children:					
Others:					
Total Members:					

(Continued)

1. Judging from their scores, which client family do you think would be better able to handle a do-it-yourself remodeling project? Why?

_____

_____

_____

_____

_____

2. Consider the family that is not as skillful to handle the project. What additional resources (either human or nonhuman) would you recommend this client family use to have a successful remodeling project? Explain how each additional resource would be helpful.

_____

_____

_____

_____

_____

3. For both client families, write which family member you think would be best suited to handle the following tasks.

	Family 1	Family 2
Making arrangements with a remodeling contractor:		
Carrying heavy supplies into the house:		
Providing moral support:		
Cleaning paintbrushes:		

4. Describe how taking an inventory of human resources can be helpful to clients.

_____

_____

_____

_____

_____

_____

_____

Decision Making

Name_____

Date_____ Period _____

Solve a housing dilemma or challenge facing your family or a family you know (without stating names) by using the decision-making process that follows.

Step 1. State the challenge. _____

_____

_____

_____

_____

_____

_____

_____

Step 2. List possible solutions._____

_____

_____

_____

_____

_____

_____

2A. What are the consequences of each solution?_____

_____

_____

_____

_____

_____

_____

_____

Step 3. Make a decision._____

_____

_____

3A. Will the outcome give lasting satisfaction? Explain. _____

_____

_____

(Continued)

Name_____

3B. Will everyone involved be satisfied? Explain. _____

_____

_____

3C. What other decisions must be made first? _____

_____

_____

Step 4. Take action. (Decide the action you would take.) _____

_____

_____

_____

_____

_____

_____

_____

_____

_____

_____

_____

_____

Step 5. Evaluate results. (What can you do to judge the effectiveness of your decision?) _____

_____

_____

_____

_____

_____

_____

_____

_____

_____

_____

_____

_____

Evaluating a Place to Live

Name _____

Date _____ Period _____

Visit a subdivision. Walk through the models and complete the following evaluation.

Name of subdivision:_____

Check off the areas below that best describe this subdivision.

Site size:

_____ Large

_____ Medium

_____ Small

Contour of the land:

_____ Level

_____ Gentle slope

_____ Steep slope

Soil characteristics:

_____ Sand

_____ Gravel

_____ Rock

_____ Clay

Lots:

_____ Attractive

_____ Unattractive

Location in community:

_____ Edge

_____ Center

Traffic:

_____ Much street traffic

_____ Little street traffic

Type of structures:

_____ Single-family

_____ Multifamily

_____ Mixed

Density of population:

_____ Sparse

_____ Crowded

Neighborhood:

_____ Residential

_____ Commercial

_____ Industrial

_____ Combination

Population composition:

_____ Homogeneous (similar)

_____ Heterogeneous (varied)

Describe the structural quality of the homes. _____

_____

_____

_____

How far are the nearest grocery store and shopping center? _____

How far is the nearest school? _____

How far is the nearest medical facility? _____

How far is the nearest recreational facility? _____

How far is the nearest fire department? _____

How far is the nearest police department? _____

What are the advantages of this subdivision? _____

What are the disadvantages of this subdivision? _____

Investigating Site Zones

Activity G   Name_____

Chapter 3   Date_____ Period_____

Use online resources to locate an image of a lot design for the house floor plan below. You may wish to include landscape walls, fences, trees, shrubs, and hedges in the lot design you choose. Insert the website link (URL) of the lot design you like. Then describe the zones within the site in the space provided following the floor plan image.

Evita Van Zoeren/Shutterstock.com

URL (website link):

_____

The *public zone* includes these areas:

_____

_____

_____

The *service zone* includes these areas:

_____

_____

_____

The *private zone* includes these areas:

_____

_____

_____

Special Housing Needs

Name_____

Date_____   Period _____

Interview a person with a physical disability—such as limited reach, mobility, hearing, or vision—to learn about his or her special housing needs. (The disability can be temporary, such as a broken leg, or permanent.) Briefly describe the person in the space below, then answer the following questions.

Description of the person:

_____

_____

_____

_____

1. What qualities about this person affect his or her housing needs?

_____

_____

_____

_____

2. In what ways are this person's special housing needs being met?

_____

_____

_____

_____

3. Which special housing needs are not being met? Why?

_____

_____

_____

_____

4. How might the principles of universal design be of benefit to this person and his or her family members? Why?

_____

_____

_____

_____

Sustainability and Housing

Sustainability and Sustainable Design

Activity A   Name_____

Chapter 4   Date _____   Period _____

In the chart that follows, write the definitions of *sustainability* and *sustainable design*. Write at least two points that support each definition in the space provided. Then respond to the items that follow the table.

Sustainability	Sustainable Design
Definition:	**Definition:**
Supporting points:	**Supporting points:**
• _____ _____ • _____ _____ • _____ _____	• _____ _____ • _____ _____ • _____ _____

1. In your own words, explain the importance of sustainability and sustainable design.

   _____

   _____

   _____

   _____

   _____

2. List and briefly summarize four eco-friendly labeling and certification programs that support sustainability and sustainable design.

   _____

   _____

   _____

   _____

   _____

Principles of Sustainable Design

Activity B

Chapter 4

Name _____

Date _____   Period _____

Complete the following graphic organizer by writing one of the principles of sustainable design in each of the outer bubbles. In the space that follows the graphic organizer, write one way you could use each principle in your home or the home of someone you know.

	Principles of Sustainable Design	

_____

_____

_____

_____

_____

_____

_____

Solar and Geothermal Energy

Name_____

Date_____ Period _____

Many people today build new homes that utilize renewable energy sources. Use the text and Internet resources to research companies that produce active solar systems and geothermal systems for housing in your community. Complete the following chart, writing the details for each in the space provided. Then answer the question that follows.

	Solar	Geothermal
Systems Available Locally		
Advantages		
Disadvantages		
Features		
Cost		
Installation Time		
Maintenance		

What factors should you consider when adapting an existing dwelling to use solar or geothermal energy?

_____

_____

_____

_____

_____

_____

Sustainability in Housing

Activity D   Name_____

Chapter 4   Date _____   Period _____

Complete the following statements by placing the missing word(s) in the space provided to the left of each number.

_____   1. Incorporating sustainability in the built environment refers to
                               _____ _____.

_____   2. Dwellings with home automation have an integrated and centrally
                               controlled system based on _____ technology.

_____   3. _____ sources of energy replenish themselves regularly.

_____   4. Only coal produces more electricity in the U.S. than _____ _____.

_____   5. An active solar system that converts the sun's energy into electricity is
                               a(n) _____ system.

_____   6. _____ energy comes from the Earth's core.

_____   7. _____ energy is another primary source of energy the United States uses
                               to produce electricity.

_____   8. An efficient, clean, and reliable approach to generating power and
                               thermal energy from a single fuel source is called _____.

_____   9. Housing and interior design professionals should choose _____
                               materials that are certified as environmentally friendly.

_____   10. _____ _____ is a key practice that promotes sustainability.

_____   11. The release of fumes and chemicals in the air as a result of the treatment
                               of a product, such as carpeting, is called _____-_____.

_____   12. _____ _____ _____ are chemicals that evaporate into the air that can
                               cause breathing difficulties and health problems for some people.

_____   13. Sponsored by the U.S. Green Building Council, the _____ certification
                               program provides sustainability guidelines for residential, commercial,
                               and other buildings.

_____   14. _____ shingles convert sunlight into electricity and resemble
                               conventional fiberglass roofing shingles.

_____   15. Wastewater from washing machines, showers, and sinks—or _____—is
                               not contaminated with human waste and can be used for landscape
                               watering.

_____   16. A home that produces and uses its own energy—as much or more than
                               it needs—is known as a _____ _____ _____.

Exterior Design Styles

Roof Styles and Housing Types

Activity A   Name _____

Chapter 5   Date _____   Period _____

Label each of the following roof styles and name a housing type on which each roof style is used. Write your responses in the space provided.

1. _____   5. _____

2. _____   6. _____

3. _____   7. _____

4. _____   8. _____

Goodheart-Willcox Publisher

Origin and Style of Traditional Houses

Activity B   Name _____

Chapter 5   Date _____ Period _____

Read each of the descriptions in the following chart. For each description, write in the origin of the house in the left column and write the housing style to which it refers in the right column.

Origin	Description	Housing Style
1. _____	These eight-sided structures are usually made of mud and logs.	_____
2. _____	Characteristics of these houses include boxlike construction, flat roofs, and projecting beams.	_____
3. _____	This small, symmetrical, one- or one-and-one-half story house with a steep gable roof and side gables has a central entrance and a central chimney. The windows are multipaned.	_____
4. _____	This house is a variation of the Cape Cod design modified with a lean-to section built on the rear of the house. It is usually two- or two-and-one-half stories in the front, but just one story in the rear. It has a steep-pitched gable roof that slants down from front to rear.	_____
5. _____	Named after forts, these structures have an overhanging second story that allows extra space on the second floor. They have steep gable roofs and windows with small panes of glass.	_____
6. _____	These asymmetrically designed dwellings contain characteristics such as a red tile roof, an enclosed patio, arch-shaped windows and doors, wrought iron exterior decor, and stucco walls.	_____
7. _____	Built on a stone or rock foundation, this one-story rectangular building, built of unfinished logs, contains at least one window and a gable roof.	_____
8. _____	These houses have a gambrel roof. Other characteristics include a central entrance, a chimney that is not centered, dormers in the second story, and windows with small panes. The houses are usually built of fieldstone or brick.	_____

(Continued)

28 *Housing and Interior Design* Workbook

Copyright Goodheart-Willcox Co., Inc.
May not be reproduced or posted to a publicly accessible website.

Name_____

Origin	Description	Housing Style
9. _____	A symmetrically styled house with a Mansard roof. It may contain dormers.	_____
10. _____	This house has a delicate, dignified appearance and is usually symmetrical. The tops of the windows break into the eave line.	_____
11. _____	These houses have simple, symmetrical exterior lines with either a hip or gable roof style. They have tall chimneys at each end of the roof.	_____
12. _____	This symmetrical house is at least two stories high with a boxlike shape. It has a flat roof surrounded by a balustrade and pediments over the porticoes, doors, or windows.	_____
13. _____	This house continued the symmetry of the Georgian style. It includes swags, garland, urns, and other motifs. The style features a fanlight over the front entrance and Palladian windows.	_____
14. _____	Monticello is an example of this style that features a large portico with columns and a triangular pediment gable.	_____
15. _____	A house of this style has a two-story entry porch supported by columns. It also has a large triangular gable with pediment. The houses are symmetrical with bold moldings and heavy cornices.	_____
16. _____	An offshoot of the Greek Revival style, this two-story house has columns that extend across the front covered by an extension of the roof. The house is large and symmetrical with a hip or gable roof.	_____
17. _____	This house style contains an abundance of decorative trim with high porches, steep gable roofs, tall windows, and a turret or small tower.	_____

Housing Styles

Activity C   Name _____

Chapter 5   Date _____ Period _____

Part 1. Describe the following housing styles in your own words. Write your descriptions in the space provided.

Traditional: _____

_____

_____

Modern: _____

_____

_____

Contemporary: _____

_____

_____

Postmodern: _____

_____

_____

Part 2. Use Internet resources to locate photo examples representing each of the housing styles. Insert the website link (URL) for your photo examples in the space provided, or attach photos representing each of these styles in the space provided. Discuss these housing styles in class.

Traditional

(Continued)

Copyright Goodheart-Willcox Co., Inc.
May not be reproduced or posted to a publicly accessible website.

Modern

Contemporary

Postmodern

Evolution of Exteriors

Activity D   Name_____

Chapter 5   Date _____   Period _____

Complete the following sentences by writing the missing word(s) in the space provided to the left of each number.

_____ 1. The Pueblo in New Mexico live in _____ houses.

_____ 2. The symmetrical _____ _____ house may be two-and-one-half stories high.

_____ 3. The Scandinavian immigrants brought the _____ _____ to North America.

_____ 4. The main features of the _____ _____ style are a two-story entry porch supported by Greek columns with a large triangular gable with a pediment.

_____ 5. The _____ _____ style with a gambrel roof was first built in New York and Delaware.

_____ 6. _____ style houses reflect the experiences and traditions of past eras.

_____ 7. The _____ style of house has an overhanging second story like the old forts.

_____ 8. The _____ style, adapted from English architecture, has simple exterior lines, a dignified appearance, and symmetry.

_____ 9. The housing styles developed in the United States from the early 1900s to the 1980s are classified as _____.

_____ 10. The Federal style sometimes has a(n) _____.

_____ 11. The _____ style developed following the American Revolution.

_____ 12. A(n) _____ is a small tower on a Victorian house.

_____ 13. The _____ house, with its lean-to section, is a variation of the Cape Cod style.

_____ 14. Haunted houses in horror movies are usually in _____ style.

_____ 15. The _____ house style allows interior space to visually flow outdoors through porches, terraces, and windows.

_____ 16. _____ houses are easy to maneuver through and maintain.

_____ 17. The architect who designed the prairie house was _____ _____ _____.

_____ 18. House styles that are the current or latest designs being constructed today are called _____.

_____ 19. Energy from the sun is used to heat _____ houses.

_____ 20. _____ -_____ houses are partially covered with soil, which makes them energy efficient since the soil is a natural insulator and helps protect the house from weather elements and climate extremes.

Alphabet of Lines

Activity A   Name_____

Chapter 6   Date_____   Period _____

Read the following descriptions of line types that commonly appear on floor plans. In the space provided to the left of each description, write the type of line described.

_____ 1. Lines that show an object continues on, but the complete view is not shown.

_____ 2. Lines that show edges of surfaces that are not visible in a specific view of a house.

_____ 3. Lines that show alternate positions, repeated details, and paths of motion.

_____ 4. Lines that show a feature has been sectioned. Another name for these lines is crosshatch lines.

_____ 5. Lines that show the outline of a building, walls, plumbing fixtures, cabinetry, and any other tangible element that can be seen in a current view. The thickness of these lines will vary depending on the importance of the object and its distance from the viewer.

_____ 6. Lines that show the extent and direction of measurements.

_____ 7. Lines that show the center of an arc or circle, for example, to indicate the location to install a ceiling fan.

Goodheart-Willcox Publisher

Floor Plan Symbols

Name_____

Date_____   Period _____

Identify these symbols, which are often used in floor plans. Write your answer in the space provided below each symbol.

1. _____   2. _____   3. _____

4. _____   5. _____   6. _____

7. _____   8. _____   9. _____

10. _____   11. _____   12. _____

13. _____   14. _____   15. _____

16. _____   17. _____   18. _____

Goodheart-Willcox Publisher

Floor Plan Evaluation

Name_____

Date _____   Period _____

The floor plan below is for the home of a married couple, both 30, with a 3-year-old child. Read their profile.

Mother: Has a full-time day job at a nearby office; enjoys reading, entertaining friends, blogging, and crafts

Father: Stay-at-home parent who operates a home-based business during the evening; enjoys playing the piano, entertaining friends, and watching television

Toddler: Likes to play with toys and have friends over for play dates; takes a nap in the afternoon; goes to bed several hours before his parents

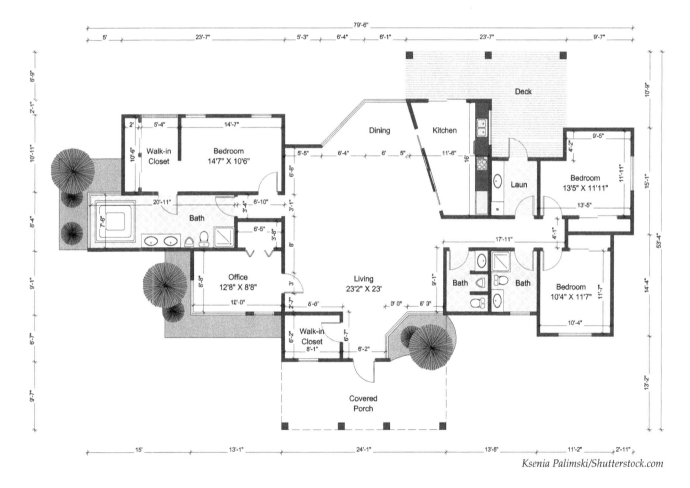

Ksenia Palimski/Shutterstock.com

For each of the following activities, examine the floor plan and describe the room or space to locate the activites. Then answer the questions that follow.

1. Working in home office _____

_____

_____

(Continued)

2. Entertaining friends _____

_____

_____

3. Playing the piano _____

_____

_____

4. Storing visitors' outerwear _____

_____

_____

5. Reading and blogging _____

_____

_____

6. Watching television _____

_____

_____

7. Storing craft supplies _____

_____

_____

8. Storing toys _____

_____

_____

9. Is the home office located so the father can work with minimal interruptions?

_____

10. Can guests enter and leave the home without walking through private areas? Why or why not?

_____

_____

11. Can the mother read or use a computer without being interrupted by sounds from the television or piano? Why or why not?

_____

_____

12. Can the child nap or sleep without being awakened by his parents' activities? Why or why not?

_____

_____

Chapter 7

Space Planning and Functionality

Identifying Functional Zones

Activity A

Chapter 7

Name _____

Date _____ Period _____

Review the floor plan below. In the chart following the floor plan, write the names of the rooms that appear in each functional zone area. Then, answer the questions that follow.

Evita Van Zoeren/Shutterstock.com

(Continued)

Private Area	Work Area	Social Area

1. In your opinion, how do the outdoor areas serve as extensions for the private, work, and social zones of this home?

_____

_____

_____

_____

_____

_____

2. What is an advantage of not separating a large area with walls? _____

_____

_____

_____

_____

_____

Circulation Activities and Traffic Patterns

Activity B

Chapter 7

Name_____

Date_____   Period _____

Part 1: In your own words, describe the special considerations to take when planning the movement throughout a living space for the following circulation activities.

1. Family:_____

_____

_____

_____

_____

_____

2. Guests: _____

_____

_____

_____

_____

_____

3. Work: _____

_____

_____

_____

_____

_____

4. Service:_____

_____

_____

_____

_____

_____

(Continued)

Part 2: Review the floor plan below. In the space that follows, describe how the traffic patterns for guests is similar to and different from the traffic patterns of household members.

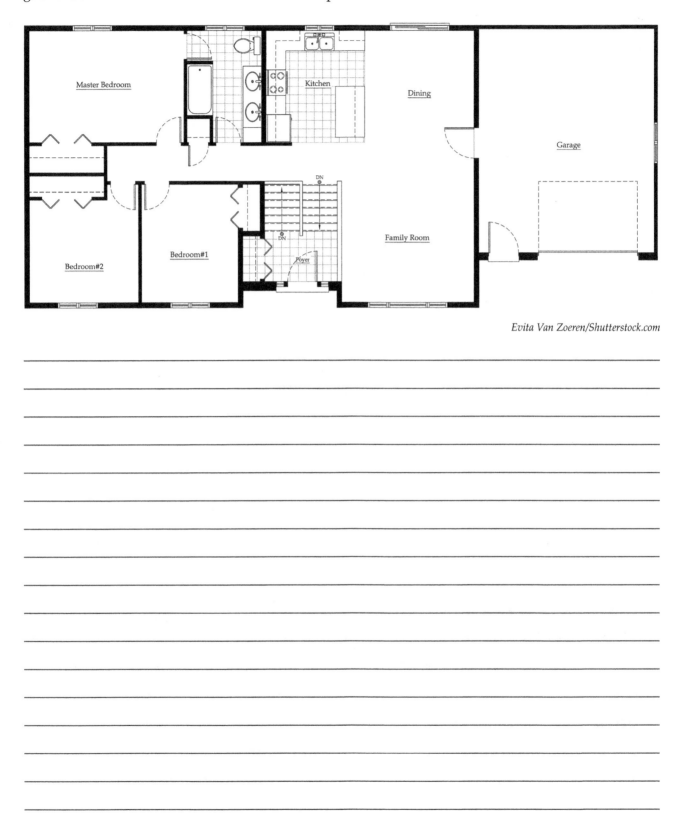

Evita Van Zoeren/Shutterstock.com

_____

_____

_____

_____

_____

_____

_____

_____

_____

_____

_____

_____

_____

_____

_____

_____

_____

_____

_____

Evaluating Clearances

Activity C   Name_____

Chapter 7   Date_____   Period _____

Evaluate the bedroom and main bath drawing below. Imagine the household member who uses this bedroom is buying new furniture. For each of the furniture items listed in the chart following the diagram, write the amount of clearance space each item will require. Use text Figure 7.15 for reference. Then answer the questions that follow.

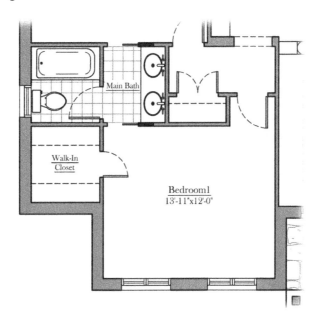

Evita Van Zoeren/Shutterstock.com

Furniture Piece	Clearance Space in Inches
Queen-size bed	
Dresser with mirror (52 inches wide by 18 inches deep)	
Wing-back chair	
Small desk with chair (32 inches wide by 24 inches deep)	

1. How much clearance space will the household member require for making the bed?

_____

2. How much circulation space will be required for the bedroom exit, closet area, and entry to the main bath?

_____

3. In your opinion, does this room have space for the amount of furniture the household member desires? Why or why not? What evidence can you give to support your reasoning?

_____

_____

_____

Space Planning and Functionality Terms

Name_____

Date_____ Period _____

Use the following terms to complete the sentences below. Write the missing word(s) in the space provided to the left of each number.

alcove   common-use storage   social area
anthropometry   functional zone   space planning
built-in storage   multipurpose room   template
circulation   private area   traffic patterns
clearance space   scale floor plan   work area

_____ 1. The process of placing furnishings for a well-functioning and visually pleasing area is _____ _____.

_____ 2. An efficient way to organize space is to group rooms by _____.

_____ 3. Bedrooms and bathrooms are examples of the _____ _____ of a house.

_____ 4. Bedrooms may become _____ _____ during active periods of the day.

_____ 5. The kitchen, laundry area, utility room, and garage are generally part of the _____ _____ of a home.

_____ 6. An area of the house that provides space for daily living, recreation, and entertaining is the _____ _____.

_____ 7. An _____ is a small recessed section of a room.

_____ 8. Family, guest, work, and service are four types of _____, or movement.

_____ 9. The paths household members use to move easily within a room, from room to room, or to the outdoors are _____ _____.

_____ 10. _____-_____ _____ includes shelves and drawers that are part of a housing structure.

_____ 11. _____-_____ _____ is used by all who live in a house.

_____ 12. _____ is the scientific study of human body measurements on a comparative basis.

_____ 13. A reduced-size drawing that is directly proportional to the actual size and shape of a space or room is a(n) _____ _____ _____.

_____ 14. A(n) _____ is a small piece of paper or plastic scaled to the actual dimensions of the furniture piece it represents.

_____ 15. A measurement term for the amount of space to leave unobstructed around furniture to allow for ease of use and good traffic pattern is a(n) _____ _____.

Planning for Individual Spaces

Terms for Planning Spaces

Activity A   Name _____

Chapter 8   Date _____ Period _____

Use the following terms to complete the sentences below. Write the missing word(s) in the space provided to the left of each number.

accessibility   hearing disability   qualitative needs
adaptability   landing space   quantitative information
adjacencies   micro-adjacencies   universal design (UD)
butler's pantry   mobility limitation   vision disability
hand limitation   physical limitation   work triangle

_____ 1. A(n) _____ _____ is a service room between the kitchen and dining room.

_____ 2. An area on either side or across from an appliance or other functional kitchen piece that serves as a space to set cooking tools is called a _____ _____.

_____ 3. A(n) _____ _____ is an imaginary line that connects the three work centers in a kitchen.

_____ 4. _____-_____ is the nearness of two or more tasks or tools within a room.

_____ 5. _____ is the nearness of two or more rooms or functions.

_____ 6. A person who has difficulty walking from one location to the other likely has a _____ _____.

_____ 7. A(n) _____ _____ results from arthritis and other conditions limiting movement and gripping ability.

_____ 8. A person with any degree of hearing loss has a(n) _____ _____.

_____ 9. A personal who is legally blind has one form of _____ _____.

_____ 10. _____ _____ is a design concept that focuses on making living environments, and the products used to create them, without special adaptation.

_____ 11. The ability to change or fit different circumstances is known as _____.

_____ 12. Mobility, vision, and hearing disabilities are known as _____ _____.

_____ 13. _____ is the ability to reach something and use it.

_____ 14. Characteristics (quality needs) of an object or interior that cannot be measured such as the need for privacy, security, and control are known as _____ _____.

_____ 15. A characteristic of an object or interior that can be measured with numbers is known as _____ _____.

Understanding the Principles of Universal Design

To better understand the *Principles of Universal Design*, search the North Carolina State University website for the Center for Universal Design. Refer to the Principles of Universal Design document as you complete the following chart.

Principle	Guidelines for Using the Principle
Principle 1: Equitable Use The design is useful and marketable to people with diverse abilities.	
Principle 2: Flexibility in Use The design accommodates a wide range of individual preferences and abilities.	
Principle 3: Simple and Intuitive Use Use of the design is easy to understand, regardless of the user's experience, knowledge, languages, skills, or current concentration level.	
Principle 4: Perceptible Information The design communicates necessary information effectively to the user, regardless of ambient conditions or the user's sensory abilities.	
Principle 5: Tolerance for Error The design minimizes hazards and the adverse consequences of accidental or unintended actions.	
Principle 6: Low Physical Effort The design can be used efficiently and comfortably and with minimum fatigue.	
Principle 7: Size and Space for Approach and Use Appropriate size and space are provided for approach, reach, manipulation, and use regardless of user's body size, posture, or mobility.	

Copyright ©1997 North Carolina State University, the Center for Universal Design (www.design.ncsu.edu/cud)

Identifying Kitchen Layouts

Name _____

Date _____   Period _____

For each of the kitchen layout diagrams that follow, list the name of the layout and an advantage and disadvantage.

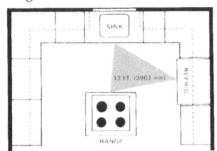

1. Kitchen layout name: _____

   Advantage:_____

   Disadvantage:_____

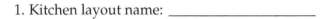

2. Kitchen layout name: _____

   Advantage:_____

   Disadvantage:_____

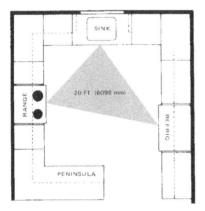

3. Kitchen layout name: _____

   Advantage:_____

   Disadvantage:_____

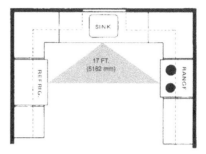

4. Kitchen layout name: _____

   Advantage:_____

   Disadvantage:_____

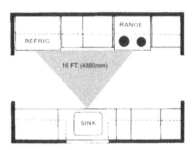

5. Kitchen layout name: _____

   Advantage:_____

   Disadvantage:_____

6. Kitchen layout name: _____

   Advantage:_____

   Disadvantage:_____

Case Study—Accessible Bathroom

Name _____

Date _____   Period _____

Presume you are a housing and interior design professional. Read the following case study and then write your responses to the items that follow in the space provided. Utilize the text and Internet resources to develop your responses.

> Your new client, Manuel (or Manny as his friends call him), is an older adult in his early 80s. Manny lives in a small, modest bungalow in a large midwestern community. Located on the first level of the home, the main full bath is small, measuring 5 feet by 9 feet and is adjacent to the master bedroom (14 feet by 16 feet). The bath contains a tub/shower combination, toilet, and a pedestal sink. The entry door is narrow at 28 inches. Due to a health condition, Manny recently began using a walker and has difficulty maneuvering in the bathroom, which lacks universal design features. Manny desires to stay in his home and wants to make some modifications to ensure accessibility and safety. Storage in the bathroom is also a concern. Manny comes to you to for help with redesigning his living space, primarily the bathroom, to accommodate his needs. The home has an additional full bath on the second floor.

1. What additional questions would you ask Manny about the space in his home and his needs?

_____

_____

_____

_____

_____

_____

_____

_____

_____

2. Based on what you know about Manny's living space, what recommendations would you make to create an accessible and safe main bath and master bedroom for Manny?

_____

_____

_____

_____

_____

_____

_____

_____

_____

Understanding Construction Basics

The House Foundation

Activity A

Chapter 9

Name_____

Date _____   Period _____

Part 1: Answer the following items about the house foundation. Write your answers in the space provided.

1. What is the house *foundation*, and of what does it consist? _____

_____

2. What is a *footing*? _____

3. What are the *foundation walls*, and what do they form? _____

_____

Part 2: Label the parts of a *slab-on-grade* foundation. Place the letter of the correct part in the space provided to the left of the part name.

Slab-on-Grade

Modern Carpentry by Wagner and Smith, Goodheart-Willcox

_____ 4. Foundation wall and footing

_____ 5. Studding

_____ 6. Brick

_____ 7. Rebar

_____ 8. Grade

_____ 9. Slab bed

_____ 10. Vapor barrier

_____ 11. Slab

(Continued)

Part 3: Label the parts of a *footing* and *foundation wall* for a basement. Place the letter of the correct part in the space provided to the left of the part name.

Footing and Foundation Wall for Basement

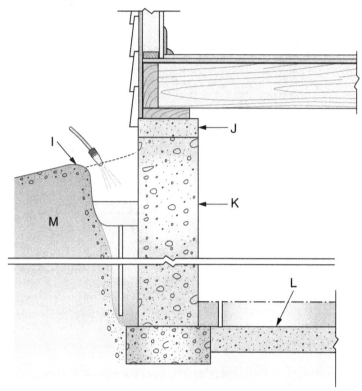

Modern Carpentry by Wagner and Smith, Goodheart-Willcox

_____ 12. Gravel fill

_____ 13. Finish grade

_____ 14. Reinforced concrete cap

_____ 15. Soil

_____ 16. Masonry wall

The House Frame

Name_____

Date_____ Period _____

Part 1: Match the letter of each part of the floor and wall framing with the correct part in the list following the image.

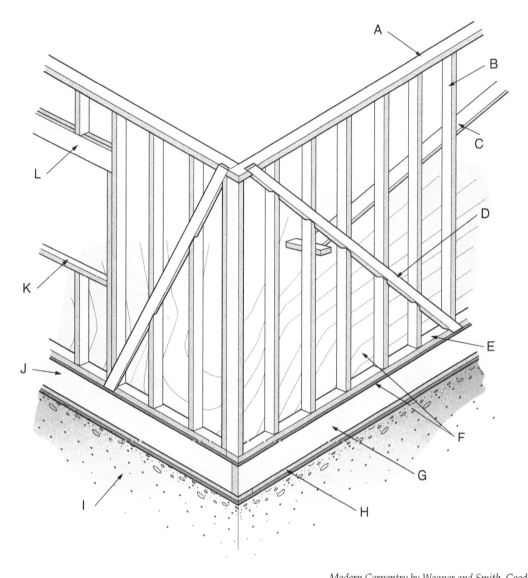

Modern Carpentry by Wagner and Smith, Goodheart-Willcox

_____ 1. Foundation wall

_____ 2. Header joist

_____ 3. Top plate

_____ 4. Stud

_____ 5. Window header

_____ 6. Temporary brace

_____ 7. Windowsill

_____ 8. Corner bracing

_____ 9. Anchored sill plate

_____ 10. Sole plate

_____ 11. Stringer joist

_____ 12. Subfloor

Name_____

Part 2: Define the following terms that are part of the floor, wall, roof, and ceiling framing of a house. Write your responses in the space provided.

13. Girder: _____

_____

_____

14. Floor joist:_____

_____

_____

15. Header: _____

_____

_____

16. Rafter:_____

_____

_____

17. Ridge: _____

_____

_____

18. Sole plate: _____

_____

_____

19. Stud: _____

_____

_____

20. Subflooring:_____

_____

_____

21. Bearing wall:_____

_____

_____

22. Nonbearing wall: _____

_____

_____

Siding Materials

Name_____

Date_____   Period _____

Complete the following chart by identifying the advantages and disadvantages of various construction materials.

Siding Material	Advantages	Disadvantages
Wood Siding		
Aluminum Siding		
Vinyl Siding		
Pressed Wood Siding		
Fiber-cement Siding		
Masonry Siding		

Choosing Windows and Doors

Activity D   Name_____

Chapter 9   Date_____   Period _____

The Morales family needs to make some decisions about windows and doors in their home. Read about their housing goals and answer the questions that follow to help them meet their needs.

1. What are three functions that everyone wants a window to provide?_____

   _____

2. To keep fuel bills down, what energy-efficient materials might the family select for the windows?

   _____

3. The family wants the front of the house to have a contemporary look. What type of windows might create this appearance?

   _____

4. Mr. Morales wants plenty of ventilation in the kitchen. What type of windows might he select for this room?

   _____

5. Mr. and Mrs. Morales want fresh air in the children's playroom in the basement. The children, however, do not always remember to close windows before leaving a room. This caused several pieces of playroom furniture to be damaged during a recent rainstorm. What type of windows might be a good choice to prevent this from happening again?

   _____

6. Mrs. Morales wants to clean windows and screens in the upstairs bedrooms without standing on a ladder outside the house. What type of windows might she select for these rooms?

   _____

7. The dining room is air conditioned, so windows are not needed for ventilation. There is a lovely view, however, outside the dining room window. The family wants the window to serve as a focal point in the room. What type of window might they select for this room?

   _____

8. The family room is located in the center of the house. Because there are no windows, the room seems rather dark. What can the family do to give the room a brighter, more airy appearance?

   _____

9. Mrs. Morales wants to install a door between the kitchen and the dining room; however, the refrigerator is located on one side of the doorway, and cabinets are mounted on the other side. This leaves little room for a door to swing open and close. What type of door might she choose for this location?

   _____

10. Mr. Morales wants the front door to provide security and serve as a weather barrier. What type of door might he choose for the front of the house?

   _____

Interior Systems

Household Plumbing and Fixtures

Activity A   Name_____

Chapter 10   Date_____   Period _____

Imagine you are a housing and interior design professional. You are helping clients select kitchen, bathroom, and laundry fixtures for their home. Use Internet resources to research vendor websites for fixtures that fit your clients' needs and wants. Your clients want you send the fixture website links for them to review. Insert the vendor website links (URLs) for the images in the space provided. Then answer the questions that the clients might have.

1. Which of the fixtures pictured require a hot water branch line? _____

_____

2. Where does the hot water main start in a house? _____

3. Why is a shutoff valve installed on each branch line next to each fixture or appliance?_____

_____

4. How do waste disposal pipes differ from water supply lines?_____

_____

5. How are gases from the wastewater removal system removed? _____

_____

6. What is the purpose of a trap in a plumbing fixture? _____

_____

_____

Heating Systems

Name_____

Date_____   Period _____

Imagine you are a heating system technician. Your clients want you to explain heating systems to them. Complete the following information to describe three different heating systems. Then decide which of these systems you would recommend to your clients for their homes and explain your reasoning.

1. Heating system: _____

   Fuel used: _____

   How is the air heated and circulated? _____

   Advantages: _____

   _____

   Disadvantages:_____

   _____

2. Heating system: _____

   Fuel used: _____

   How is the air heated and circulated? _____

   Advantages: _____

   _____

   Disadvantages:_____

   _____

3. Heating system: _____

   Fuel used: _____

   How is the air heated and circulated? _____

   Advantages: _____

   _____

   Disadvantages:_____

   _____

My recommendation of a heating system is _____

My reasons for recommending this system for my clients are _____

_____

_____

Energy Savvy

Name_____

Date_____   Period _____

Imagine you are a columnist for "Energy Savvy" magazine. You have been assigned to write home energy conservation tips for an article. Write an introductory paragraph and then using the text and current Internet and print resources, list energy tips under the headings below. Use the text and Internet or print resources for your research.

_____

_____

_____

_____

General Tips

_____

_____

_____

_____

_____

Windows and Doors

_____

_____

_____

_____

_____

Sealing and Insulation

_____

_____

_____

_____

_____

Computerized Devices

_____

_____

_____

_____

_____

Targeted Air Sealing

_____

_____

_____

_____

_____

Conserving Water

_____

_____

_____

_____

_____

Terms for Interior Systems

Name_____

Date_____   Period _____

Complete the following sentences by writing the missing word(s) in the space provided.

_____ 1. A _____ is a interdependent group of items forming a unified whole.

_____ 2. Another name for electricity is _____ _____.

_____ 3. Usually a wire, the _____ allows the flow of electricity.

_____ 4. When electrons follow a path from the source of electricity to the device and back to the source, a _____ forms.

_____ 5. The measure of the amount of electricity passing through a conductor per unit of time is the _____.

_____ 6. _____ is the measure of the pressure used to push the electrical current along a conductor.

_____ 7. The amount of electrical power used is measured in _____.

_____ 8. A metal or plastic pipe that protects electrical wires is called _____.

_____ 9. A _____ _____ contains the wires connecting the utility pole transformer to the point of entry to a customer's home.

_____ 10. A _____ monitors electrical usage.

_____ 11. A(n) _____ _____ _____ protects each circuit by stopping the excessive flow of electrical current in a circuit.

_____ 12. A switch that automatically trips and interrupts the flow of electrical current in the event of an abnormal condition is called a _____.

_____ 13. A special electrical device that stops the flow of electrical current in a circuit as a safety precaution is a _____ _____ _____.

_____ 14. _____ _____ can turn on automatically to create electricity when the electric power fails.

_____ 15. A vertical pipe that extends through the roof to release gases and odors outdoors is called a _____ _____.

_____ 16. The main vertical pipe that receives waste matter from all plumbing fixtures is the _____ _____.

_____ 17. A _____ is a bend in the pipe just below a plumbing fixture that catches and holds water to prevent sewage gas from seeping back into the house.

_____ 18. An acronym for heating, ventilating, and air-conditioning is _____.

_____ 19. A type of furnace that heats and delivers the air to rooms is called a _____ _____-_____ _____.

_____ 20. A large, round tube or rectangular boxlike structure that delivers heated air to distant rooms or spaces is called a _____.

_____ 21. _____ restricts the flow of air between the house interior and the outdoors.

_____ 22. _____ _____ is material that covers the edges of a window or door to prevent moisture and air from entering the house.

Chapter 11

Lighting Considerations

Understanding Lightbulbs

Activity A   Name_____

Chapter 11   Date_____   Period _____

Write the name of the parts for the incandescent and compact fluorescent lamps in the space provided. Then answer the questions that follow.

U.S. Department of Energy   *Provided by ENERGY STAR at www.energystar.gov*

1. _____   5. _____   9. _____

2. _____   6. _____   10. _____

3. _____   7. _____   11. _____

4. _____   8. _____

12. How does an incandescent bulb function to produce light? How is it efficient or inefficient?

_____

_____

_____

13. How does a compact fluorescent lamp (CFL) function to produce light? How is it efficient or inefficient?

_____

_____

_____

14. What safety considerations apply to CFLs? _____

_____

Lighting for Safety

Name_____

Date_____   Period _____

Evaluate the following floor plan for light-switch locations. Then list the location(s) of light switches for each room in the space provided. Write a *yes* or *no* in the space provided in the checklist to evaluate your placement of light switches. Write other steps you can take to ensure lighting promotes safety.

1st Floor

2nd Floor

Evita Van Zoeren/Shutterstock.com

1. Kitchen: _____

2. Dining: _____

3. Great room: _____

4. Master bedroom: _____

5. Master bath: _____

6. Guest bedroom: _____

7. Bathroom, 2nd floor: _____

8. Loft: _____

9. Stairway, top: _____

10. Stairway, bottom: _____

Safety Checklist

Yes/No	Safety Items
	Are entrances well lit?
	Can you light your way as you move from room to room?
	Can room lighting be switched on or off from each doorway?
	Can stairway lighting be controlled from both the top and bottom of the stairs?
	Can outside lighting be controlled from inside the house?

What other steps can you take to ensure lighting promotes safety? _____

_____

_____

_____

Structural and Nonstructural Lighting

Activity C   Name_____

Chapter 11   Date _____   Period _____

Look for examples of lighting using online vendor catalogs. List the website links (URLs) for two examples of nonstructural lighting and three examples of structural lighting in the place provided in the chart (or attach image of each to a print copy). Then analyze the lighting by providing the information requested.

Nonstructural Lighting—Example 1 URL: _____	Lighting type:_____ Type of light provided (check all that apply): _____ diffused light _____ general lighting _____ direct lighting _____ indirect lighting _____ task lighting _____ lighting for safety _____ accent lighting Room(s) appropriate for this type of lighting: _____ _____
Nonstructural Lighting—Example 2 URL: _____	Lighting type:_____ Type of light provided (check all that apply): _____ diffused light _____ general lighting _____ direct lighting _____ indirect lighting _____ task lighting _____ lighting for safety _____ accent lighting Room(s) appropriate for this type of lighting: _____ _____

(Continued)

Structural Lighting—Example 1 URL: _____	Lighting type:_____ Type of light provided (check all that apply): _____ diffused light _____ general lighting _____ direct lighting _____ indirect lighting _____ task lighting _____ lighting for safety _____ accent lighting Room(s) appropriate for this type of lighting: _____
Structural Lighting—Example 2 URL: _____	Lighting type:_____ Type of light provided (check all that apply): _____ diffused light _____ general lighting _____ direct lighting _____ indirect lighting _____ task lighting _____ lighting for safety _____ accent lighting Room(s) appropriate for this type of lighting: _____
Structural Lighting—Example 3 URL: _____	Lighting type:_____ Type of light provided (check all that apply): _____ diffused light _____ general lighting _____ direct lighting _____ indirect lighting _____ task lighting _____ lighting for safety _____ accent lighting Room(s) appropriate for this type of lighting: _____

Selecting Appliances and Electronics

Selecting Major Appliances

Activity A   Name_____

Chapter 12   Date _____   Period _____

Locate a major appliance and its description on a manufacturer website. List the vendor website link (URL) in the space provided and write a description of the appliance features. Then write eight questions that will help a person carefully select a new one, relating your questions to the chosen appliance. In addition, write the answers to your appliance questions in the space provided.

Appliance URL: _____

Appliance description: _____

_____

_____

_____

_____

Appliance Questions

1. _____

2. _____

3. _____

4. _____

5. _____

6. _____

7. _____

8. _____

Answers to Appliance Questions

1. _____

2. _____

3. _____

4. _____

5. _____

6. _____

7. _____

8. _____

Comparing Refrigerator Costs

Activity B

Name_____

Chapter 12

Date_____   Period_____

View the websites of three businesses selling new appliances. Choose a refrigerator-freezer from each business that is one style: *top-freezer, bottom-freezer,* or *side-by-side.* At least one should be an ENERGY STAR model. Complete the information in the chart for each refrigerator. Then answer the questions that follow. Insert the website link (URL) of the EnergyGuide label for each in the space provided in the table.

	Refrigerator #1	Refrigerator #2	Refrigerator #3
Retailer Name			
Brand Name			
Model Number			
ENERGY STAR (yes or no)			
URL for EnergyGuide Label			
Estimated Yearly Operating Cost (from EnergyGuide label)	$	$	$
Price (before tax)	$	$	$
Delivery Charge	$	$	$

Which refrigerator has the least expensive purchase price (before taxes)? _____

_____

Which refrigerator is the least expensive when delivery cost is added to the purchase price?_____

_____

If the average lifespan of a refrigerator is 14 years, calculate the cost of operating each refrigerator over its lifespan.

    Refrigerator #1 $ _____

    Refrigerator #2 $ _____

    Refrigerator #3 $ _____

Which refrigerator is the least expensive when the lifespan operating cost is added to purchase price and delivery cost?

_____

_____

Is the refrigerator that is the least expensive to operate an ENERGY STAR model? _____

_____

Microwave Ovens

Activity C   Name_____

Chapter 12   Date_____   Period _____

Search online catalogs and appliance sellers to identify two models of microwave ovens. For each oven, find information about the features listed below and fill in the spaces. Then answer the questions that follow.

	Model 1	Model 2
1. Manufacturer	_____	_____
2. Style	_____	_____
3. Oven capacity	_____	_____
4. Oven wattage	_____	_____
5. Number of power levels	_____	_____
6. Automatic programming	_____	_____
7. Automatic settings	_____	_____
8. Sensor cooking	_____	_____
9. Browning element	_____	_____
10. Temperature probe or food sensor	_____	_____
11. Turntable	_____	_____
12. Microwave cookbook	_____	_____

Which features do you consider most important in a microwave oven? Why?_____

_____

_____

_____

_____

Which of the models described above do you prefer? Why? _____

_____

_____

_____

_____

_____

Washers and Dryers

Activity D   Name_____

Chapter 12   Date_____   Period _____

Obtain use-and-care manuals for a clothes washer and a dryer from home, from an appliance store, or by visiting the website of an appliance manufacturer or seller. Use the manuals to fill out the checklists and answer the questions that follow. For the checklists, place **Y** in the blanks for *yes* and **N** for *no*.

Checklist for Automatic Washers

_____   Will the washer fit your space limitations?

_____   Does the washer have a self-cleaning lint filter?

_____   Is a water-level selector provided if the model is top-loading?

_____   Is a water temperature selector provided?

_____   Does it have a minimum of regular, delicate, and permanent press cycles?

_____   Is a presoak cycle available?

_____   Is an option for heavy-duty loads available?

_____   Does it have a control to stop the machine and signal when the load is unbalanced?

_____   Does it have dispensers for detergent, bleach, and fabric softener?

_____   Is an optional second rinse selector provided?

_____   Are the tub and lid made of porcelain enamel or stainless steel?

_____   Is it an energy-efficient model?

_____   Is it a water-efficient model?

What other information in the manual would help you decide about purchasing this washer? Explain.

_____

_____

_____

_____

_____

_____

_____

_____

_____

_____

_____

_____

(Continued)

Name_____

Checklist for Dryers

_____ Is the lint trap conveniently placed for ease in removing, cleaning, and replacing?

_____ Is the control panel lighted? the interior?

_____ Is there a signal (buzzer or bell) at the end of the drying period?

_____ Is there a safety button to start the dryer?

_____ Does the dryer offer one heat setting or a choice of settings?

_____ Does it have an automatic sensor to prevent overdrying?

_____ Does the dryer offer a steam setting and moisture sensor to keep clothes fresh and reduce wrinkling?

_____ Does it offer a wrinkle-guard feature? an air-only or no-heat setting?

_____ Does it have a touch-up cycle to remove creases in dry clothes?

_____ Is it an energy-efficient model?

What other information in the manual would help you decide about purchasing this dryer? Explain.

_____

_____

_____

_____

_____

_____

_____

_____

_____

_____

_____

_____

Appliance Terms

Name_____

Date_____   Period _____

Complete the following statements by placing the missing word(s) in the space provided to the left of each number. Use each of the following terms once.

appliances	EnergyGuide label	kilowatt hour (kWh)
British thermal units (Btus)	extended warranty	limited warranty
convection ovens	full warranty	microwave ovens
dehumidifier	humidifier	self-cleaning ovens
ENERGY STAR® label	induction cooktops	warranty

_____ 1. Devices powered by gas or electricity that serve a specific use or function—and may be large or small—are called _____.

_____ 2. A _____ _____ is a unit of measure to determine energy use per hour.

_____ 3. The _____ _____ states the average yearly energy use and operating cost of an appliance.

_____ 4. Although not required, the _____ _____ _____ serves as an easy-to-use energy guide for consumers.

_____ 5. A _____ is a manufacturer's written promise that a product will meet certain performance and quality standards as outlined in written documentation.

_____ 6. A _____ _____ provides the consumer with free repair or replacement of a product or part if any defect occurs in the given time period.

_____ 7. A warrantor provides service, repairs, and replacements only under certain conditions with a _____ _____.

_____ 8. Many times, a(n) _____ _____ is not a wise purchase.

_____ 9. _____ _____ use a magnetic field below a glass-ceramic surface to generate heat in the bottom of cookware.

_____ 10. The energy usage of gas burners is measured in _____ _____ _____.

_____ 11. Extremely high temperatures are used to burn away splatters and spills in _____-_____ _____.

_____ 12. _____ _____ bake foods in a stream of heated air.

_____ 13. _____ _____ cook food with high-frequency energy waves.

_____ 14. A(n) _____ is an appliance that removes moisture from the air.

_____ 15. A(n) _____ is an appliance that adds moisture to the air.

The Outdoor Living Environment

Landscape Client Description

Activity A

Chapter 13

Name_____

Date_____   Period _____

Presume you have a new client who wants to redesign the family's outdoor living space. The family has four members, including children and an older adult family member. Create a client description of the household based on a family you know. Write your answers in the space provided.

Write a one-sentence description of the household: _____

_____

Write a brief profile of each member of the household. (*Note:* Do not use names.) Attach a page if you need additional writing space.

Member 1: _____

_____

_____

Member 2: _____

_____

_____

Member 3: _____

_____

_____

Member 4: _____

_____

_____

If you were designing an outdoor area for this household, what questions and concerns might you have based on their profiles? Write at least five questions.

_____

_____

_____

_____

_____

_____

Identify Landscape Elements

Name_____

Date_____ Period _____

Use the Internet to locate an image of a landscaped area you find pleasing. Write the website address (URL) in the space provided. Then, write a description of the area. In the chart below your description, identify the natural and manufactured elements in the illustration.

URL for landscaped image: _____

Landscape description:_____

_____

_____

_____

_____

_____

_____

_____

_____

_____

_____

Natural Landscape Elements	Manufactured Landscape Elements
_____	_____
_____	_____
_____	_____
_____	_____
_____	_____
_____	_____
_____	_____
_____	_____
_____	_____
_____	_____
_____	_____
_____	_____
_____	_____

Recommend Landscape Accents

Activity C   Name_____

Chapter 13   Date_____   Period_____

Accents in a landscape are the finishing touches. Use the Internet to locate an image of a landscaped site. Write the website link (URL) in the space provided along with a description of the landscaped site. (Attach a copy of the image to the print activity if desired.) Identify the accents used within the site. Then list five suggestions to follow when choosing accents.

URL: _____

Landscape description: _____

Accents used in the landscape: _____

_____

_____

_____

_____

_____

Suggestions to follow when choosing landscape accents:

1. _____

_____

_____

2. _____

_____

_____

3. _____

_____

_____

4. _____

_____

_____

5. _____

_____

_____

Analyze Outdoor Furnishings

Name_____

Date_____   Period _____

Use the Internet to locate three photos or advertisements for various types of outdoor furnishings. For each example, complete the information in the chart that follows.

Example 1	
URL for Image	
Type of Furnishing	
Materials Used	
Quality Features	
Uses	
Disadvantages	
Example 2	
URL for Image	
Type of Furnishing	
Materials Used	
Quality Features	
Uses	
Disadvantages	
Example 3	
URL for Image	
Type of Furnishing	
Materials Used	
Quality Features	
Uses	
Disadvantages	

Landscaping for Conservation

Activity E   Name _____

Chapter 13   Date _____   Period _____

Suppose your new client—a middle-income family—is building a new ranch-style home that is 1,200 square feet. The family is concerned about installing landscape materials that conserve water, soil, and energy. For each of the following, write five recommendations for conservation based on the climate and soil, water, and energy availability in your area. Use the text and Internet resources for reference.

Water Conservation

1. _____
   _____

2. _____
   _____

3. _____
   _____

4. _____
   _____

5. _____
   _____

Soil Conservation

6. _____
   _____

7. _____
   _____

8. _____
   _____

9. _____
   _____

10. _____
    _____

Energy Conservation

11. _____
    _____

12. _____
    _____

13. _____
    _____

14. _____
    _____

15. _____
    _____

Outdoor Living Environment Terms

Activity F   Name_____

Chapter 13   Date _____   Period _____

Complete the following statements by placing the missing word(s) in the space provided to the left of each number. Use each of the following terms once.

annuals	landscape	perennials
biennials	landscape architect	soil conservation
conservation	landscape zones	sunroom
enclosure elements	manufactured landscape	water conservation
ground cover	elements	xeriscape
hardscape	natural landscape elements	

_____ 1. The outdoor living space is also called the ____.

_____ 2. Items found in the natural environment are ____ ____ ____.

_____ 3. Flowers that must be replanted every year are ____.

_____ 4. Flowers that must be replanted every two years are ____.

_____ 5. Flowers that last for many years without replanting are ____.

_____ 6. Grasses and various types of low-growing plants are called ____ ____.

_____ 7. Boulders, stones, and anything in the landscape other than vegetation and outdoor furniture is called the ____.

_____ 8. Those elements not found in the natural environment are called ____ ____ ____.

_____ 9. Walls and fences are ____ ____ that help keep children and pets in a secure place.

_____ 10. Just as indoor divisions of a home relate to certain activities, the exterior grounds of the home have three divisions, or ____ ____.

_____ 11. ____ is the process of protecting or saving something.

_____ 12. ____ ____ includes reducing water use and eliminating water waste.

_____ 13. A landscaping method that utilizes water-conserving techniques, especially in arid or semi-arid climates, is called ____.

_____ 14. Improving and maintaining the soil is known as ____ ____.

_____ 15. A garden room, or ____, is a structure that can use energy more efficiently.

_____ 16. A professional trained to create outdoor designs that function well and are aesthetically pleasing is called a ____ ____.

Chapter 14

Elements of Design

Interior Product Characteristics

Activity A   Name_____

Chapter 14   Date_____   Period _____

Imagine a new product you might create for use in the interior design of a space. Carefully consider the function, construction, and aesthetics of your design. In the space that follows, write a word picture that communicates details about your product. Then answer the questions that follow.

Word picture of product:_____

_____

_____

_____

_____

_____

_____

_____

1. What is the name of your product? _____

2. What will your product do, or how will it be used? _____

   _____

3. To what ages, sizes, and ability levels does this product appeal?_____

   _____

   _____

4. From what materials will your product be made?_____

   _____

5. Why did you choose these particular materials? _____

   _____

   _____

6. Why do you think your potential customers will be pleased with this product? _____

   _____

   _____

Line

Name_____

Date_____ Period _____

Part 1: Identify each type of line used in housing and interior design. Write the name of the line type in the space provided below each line.

1. _____   2. _____

3. _____   4. _____

Part 2: Write the definition of *line* in the space provided. Then complete the items that follow.

5. Define *line*: _____

_____

Different types of lines create different emotional responses. Indicate the feelings or emotions produced by each of the following types of lines:

6. Horizontal:_____

7. Vertical: _____

8. Diagonal:_____

9. Curved: _____

10. List three ways to use lines in housing and interior design decisions.

_____

_____

_____

_____

_____

Form

Activity C   Name_____

Chapter 14   Date_____   Period _____

Part 1: Use the Internet to locate an image example of each of the following types of form. Write the website link (URL) in the space provided after each type of form and write a brief description of the image.

1. Realistic form:_____

   _____

   _____

2. Abstract form:_____

   _____

   _____

3. Geometric form:_____

   _____

   _____

4. Free form: _____

   _____

   _____

Part 2: Write your responses to the following items in the space provided.

5. List the three guidelines for using form in design. Give an example of each guideline.

   A. _____

      _____

      Example: _____

      _____

   B. _____

      _____

      Example: _____

      _____

   C. _____

      _____

      Example: _____

      _____

Space and Mass

Name_____

Date_____   Period _____

In the space provided, answer the following questions about space and mass as elements of design.

1. Define *space*._____

_____

2. What is the size of the space in a room of your home?

   Height:_____   Length:_____   Width:_____

3. Who uses this space?_____

_____

4. How is this space used? _____

_____

5. What feelings does this space create? _____

_____

6. How can you use space in housing and interiors to create a feeling of grandeur?_____

_____

_____

7. How can you use space in housing and interiors to create a cozy feeling? _____

_____

8. Define *mass*. _____

_____

9. How do space and mass relate to form?_____

_____

_____

10. Use the Internet to locate interior design illustrations that represent high mass and low mass. Write the website links (URLs) and a brief description of each illustration in the chart that follows.

	Website Link (URL)	**Description**
High Mass		
Low Mass		

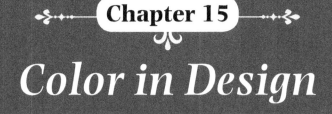

Chapter 15
Color in Design

Psychological Effects of Color

Activity A   Name_____

Chapter 15   Date_____   Period _____

Part 1: In the space provided, describe how each color in the following list makes you feel. Then answer the questions below. Compare your responses with those of others in the class.

Red:_____

_____

Orange: _____

_____

Yellow:_____

_____

Green:_____

_____

Blue: _____

_____

Violet:_____

_____

Black: _____

_____

White:_____

_____

Part 2: Considering your responses to each of the colors above and their psychological impact and meaning, if you were an interior designer, which color would you choose as the main color for a bedroom? Why?

_____

Which color would you recommend to a client for a game room? Why?_____

_____

Which color would you *not* recommend for a dining room? Why?_____

_____

Understanding the Color Wheel

Name_____

Date_____   Period _____

Part 1: Complete the following statements by writing the missing term (primary, secondary, or tertiary) in the space provided to the left of each number.

_____   1. By mixing, lightening, and darkening the _____ colors, all other colors can be made.

_____   2. Mixing equal amounts of any two primary colors produces a _____ color.

_____   3. The _____ colors are named after the two colors used to make them, with the primary color listed first.

_____   4. Red-orange, yellow-orange, yellow-green, blue-green, blue-violet, and red-violet are _____ colors.

_____   5. Red, yellow, and blue are the _____ colors.

_____   6. Green, orange, and violet are _____ colors.

Part 2: Write the letter of the correct color name in the space provided to the left of each hue.

_____ 7. Red

_____ 8. Blue

_____ 9. Yellow

_____ 10. Red-orange

_____ 11. Red-violet

_____ 12. Blue-violet

_____ 13. Blue-green

_____ 14. Yellow-green

_____ 15. Yellow-orange

_____ 16. Green

_____ 17. Orange

_____ 18. Violet

Goodheart-Willcox Publisher

Color Harmonies

Activity C

Chapter 15

Name_____

Date_____   Period _____

Match one color harmony and one color combination to each of the following descriptions. Write the appropriate letters in the spaces provided. Then use the chart below to describe two different color harmonies. Write the website links (URLs) of two photo examples of your color harmonies in the chart.

Harmony   Colors   **Description:**

_____ / _____   1. The simplest color harmony based on tints and shades of a single hue.

_____ / _____   2. A color harmony made by combining two colors opposite each other on the color wheel; sometimes called *contrasting colors*.

_____ / _____   3. A color harmony consisting of one hue with the two hues adjacent to its complement.

_____ / _____   4. A color harmony consisting of two colors and their complements.

_____ / _____   5. A color harmony created by combining related hues—those next to each other on the color wheel.

_____ / _____   6. A color harmony created by combining any three colors that are equally distant from each other on a standard color wheel.

_____ / _____   7. A color harmony using combinations of hues not on the standard color wheel.

Color Harmonies   **Color Combinations**

A. analogous color harmony   H. black, white, gray

B. complementary color harmony   I. light blue, medium blue, dark blue

C. double-complementary color harmony   J. orange, blue

D. monochromatic color harmony   K. red, orange, green, blue

E. neutral color harmonies   L. red-violet, yellow-orange, blue-green

F. split-complementary color harmony   M. violet, yellow-orange, yellow-green

G. triadic color harmony   N. yellow, yellow-green, green

Color Harmony 1	Color Harmony 2
Example (URL): _____	Example (URL): _____
Name of color harmony: _____	Name of color harmony: _____
Colors used: _____	Colors used: _____

Color Terms

Complete the following sentences by writing the missing word(s) in the space provided to the left of each number.

_____ 1. _____ is an element or a property of light.

_____ 2. The full range of all existing colors is called the _____ _____.

_____ 3. The _____ _____ is a particular circular arrangement of primary, secondary, and tertiary colors; the basis of all color relationships.

_____ 4. The _____ _____ are the colors of yellow, red, and blue from which all other colors are made.

_____ 5. The _____ _____ are the colors of orange, green, and violet; made by mixing equal amounts of two primary colors.

_____ 6. The _____ _____ are the colors made by mixing equal amounts of a primary color with a secondary color adjacent to it on the color wheel; also called *intermediate colors*.

_____ 7. _____ is the name of a color in its purest form with no added black, gray, or white.

_____ 8. _____ is the relative lightness or darkness of a hue.

_____ 9. A(n) _____ is the addition of white to a hue to make it a lighter value.

_____ 10. A(n) _____ is the addition of black to a hue to make it a darker value.

_____ 11. A(n) _____ is the result of adding gray to a hue.

_____ 12. _____ is the brightness or dullness of a hue.

_____ 13. A(n) _____ is a hue that is directly across from another hue on the color wheel.

_____ 14. A(n) _____ is a coloring agent used in paint and printed materials.

_____ 15. _____ _____ are red, yellow, and orange and the colors near them on the color wheel; also called *advancing colors*.

_____ 16. _____ _____ are blue, green, and violet and the colors near them on the color wheel; also called *receding colors*.

_____ 17. A pleasing combination of colors based on their respective positions on the color wheel is _____ _____.

_____ 18. The combination of colors selected for the design of a room or house is the _____ _____.

Principles of Design

Golden Guidelines

Activity A   Name_____

Chapter 16   Date_____   Period _____

Answer the questions that follow about the illustrations. Write your responses in the space provided.

1. In what country did the golden guidelines originate? _____

2. Which of the fireplaces at the right do you find more visually appealing?

   _____

   Why?_____

   _____

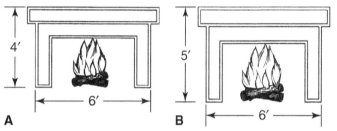

Goodheart-Willcox Publisher; Les Perysty/Shutterstock.com

3. Which of the golden guidelines is illustrated by fireplace A?

   _____

4. Which of the lamps at the right do you find most visually appealing?

   _____

   Why?_____

   _____

   _____

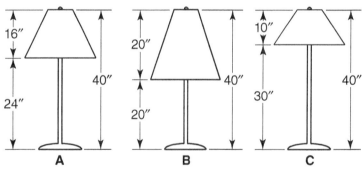

Goodheart-Willcox Publisher

5. Which of the golden guidelines is illustrated by lamp A?

   _____

6. Which of the picture placements at the right do you find more visually appealing?

   _____

   Why?_____

   _____

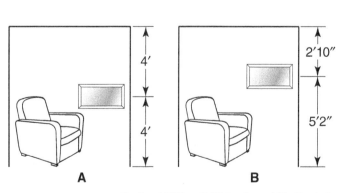

Goodheart-Willcox Publisher; bmnark/Shutterstock.com

7. Which of the golden guidelines is illustrated by picture placement B?

   _____

The Principle of Rhythm

Name_____

Date _____   Period _____

Write the type of rhythm illustrated by each of the window treatments in the images that follow. Briefly explain each type of rhythm in the space provided.

penphoto/Shutterstock.com

1. _____

   _____

   _____

Goodheart-Willcox Publisher

2. _____

   _____

   _____

Goodheart-Willcox Publisher

3. _____

   _____

   _____

Goodheart-Willcox Publisher

4. _____

   _____

   _____

Kamenuka/Shutterstock.com

5. _____

   _____

   _____

Using the Principles of Design

Name_____

Date _____ Period _____

Carefully analyze the following image. In the space provided, briefly describe how the principles of design are used in the room.

Ilya Bolotov/Shutterstock.com

Proportion and scale: _____

_____

_____

Balance: _____

_____

_____

Emphasis:_____

_____

_____

Rhythm: _____

_____

_____

Design Questions

Name_____

Date_____   Period _____

Write a question for each of the following answers based on the content of Chapter 16. In teams, take turns asking the questions in random order. See how many team members can answer the questions correctly without looking at the worksheet.

1. Proportion and scale, balance, emphasis, and rhythm. _____

_____

2. The ratio of one part to another part or of one part to the whole. _____

_____

3. The golden mean, the golden section, and the golden rectangle. _____

_____

4. The relative size of an object in relation to other objects. _____

_____

5. Thick lines, bold colors, coarse textures, and large patterns. _____

_____

6. Informal balance._____

_____

7. Picture windows, fireplaces, colorful rugs, striking works of art, and mirrors are common examples.

_____

_____

8. A type of rhythm that is created when an element of design is repeated._____

_____

9. A type of rhythm that is created by a gradual increase or decrease of similar elements of design.

_____

_____

10. Function and appropriateness, harmony with unity and variety, and beauty._____

_____

11. The result of all parts of a design related by a design idea._____

_____

12. The application of design in regard to the senses of sight, hearing, smell, and touch. _____

_____

Chapter 17

The Process of Design

Creating a Residential Client Profile

Activity A   Name _____

Chapter 17   Date _____   Period _____

Read the following residential client profile. In the space provided, create a profile of your own household or the household of someone you know.

Example: A three-generation family consisting of parents with one teen and a grandparent.

Member 1:   A 55-year-old father; a high school teacher; drives his own car; enjoys playing guitar, cooking, golfing, and watching television; needs a quiet place to grade papers.

Member 2:   A 50-year-old mother; an insurance company executive; works part-time at a nearby office and part-time from a home office; drives her own car; enjoys yoga, reading, and playing cards with friends.

Member 3:   A 15-year-old high school student; enjoys entertaining friends, rock climbing, and playing computer games; plans to buy a used car in the next few years; needs a quiet place to study.

Member 4:   An 80-year-old woman; enjoys listening to music, doing crossword puzzles, watching television, and gardening; walks with a cane.

Write a one-sentence description of the household: _____

_____

Write a brief profile of each member of the household. (*Note:* Do not use names.)

Member 1: _____

_____

_____

Member 2: _____

_____

_____

Member 3: _____

_____

_____

Member 4: _____

_____

_____

Visiting a Client's Home

Activity B

Chapter 17

Name _____

Date _____ Period _____

Make an appointment to visit the home of someone you know. Let your "client" know that you will walk through their entire living space. As you walk through the home, answer the following questions in the space provided.

1. How many rooms are there in the home? How are they arranged? _____

   _____

   _____

   _____

2. Where are the private, social, and work areas located? _____

   _____

   _____

   _____

3. What are the client's color preferences? _____

   _____

   _____

   _____

4. What are ceiling, wall, and flooring backgrounds? (For example, are walls painted or are wall coverings used? Are floors carpeted, hardwood, or something else?)

   _____

   _____

   _____

5. What style (traditional, contemporary, or eclectic, for example) is reflected in the surroundings? Include descriptions of the style of furnishings.

   _____

   _____

   _____

6. Describe any cultural artifacts in the home. _____

   _____

   _____

   _____

(Continued)

7. Make note of any features or furniture that interrupt good traffic flow. Can you walk easily from one room to the next, from one part of a room to another? If not, why not?

_____

_____

_____

8. Describe the lighting. If you visit during the day, is natural light sufficient? Is artificial lighting sufficient? Why or why not?

_____

_____

_____

9. Describe the storage areas. Are closets and storage areas for clothes, bed, and bath linens adequate? Is kitchen storage adequate? Do children's toys, sports equipment, musical instruments, or anything else require special storage?

_____

_____

_____

10. Note energy needs. Is the house sufficiently cool if the weather is warm, or is it sufficiently warm if the weather is cold? Are intake and outflow vents unobstructed? Are appliances older or newer energy-efficient models?

_____

_____

_____

After you leave the home, assess how you felt as you walked through it. What contributed to these feelings? (For example, did you feel relaxed, excited, or anxious, and why?) How would these feelings contribute to design recommendations you might make to a client?

_____

_____

_____

_____

_____

_____

_____

_____

_____

_____

Developing and Revising a Preliminary Budget

Name_____

Date _____   Period _____

A client wants to remodel a kitchen for $25,000. Many of the materials and labor requirements are listed in the following chart. (*Note:* Actual costs, especially labor costs, vary depending on your location and many other factors.) Fill in the estimated cost blanks. You can find these costs by visiting home improvement stores, searching the Internet, or by contacting local contractors. For this exercise, do not include taxes and other indirect costs. Give amounts rounded up to the nearest dollar.

Item	Description	Quantity	Estimated Cost
Porcelain Tile Floor			
Porcelain floor tiles	12 in. × 12 in.	130 tiles	$ _____
Installation (labor)			$ _____
Ceiling and Walls			
Wall paint	Taupe, flat latex	1 gal.	$ _____
Ceiling paint	White, flat latex	2 qt.	$ _____
Trim paint	Ivory, semi-gloss oil-base	1 qt.	$ _____
Painter (labor)			$ _____
Refrigerator	Side-by-side, stainless steel, free-standing, ENERGY STAR qualified	1	$ _____
Delivery/Installation/Haul away			$ _____
Range	Gas, stainless steel, slide-in style	1	$ _____
Delivery/Installation/Haul away			$ _____
Microwave	Full size, stainless steel, over-the-range style	1	$ _____
Delivery/Installation/Haul away			$ _____
Dishwasher	Tall tub style, stainless steel, ENERGY STAR qualified	1	$ _____
Delivery/Installation/Haul away			$ _____
Countertop			
Counter	Granite	20 ft.	$ _____
Installation (labor)			$ _____

(Continued)

Cabinets			
Matching special order cabinets	30 in. wide × 12 in. deep, oak, stained finish, wall cabinets	5	$ _____
	30 in. wide × 24 in. deep, oak, stained finish, base cabinets	5	$ _____
Installation (labor)			$ _____
Freight			$ _____
Window Treatments			
Special order shutters	36 in. long × 33 in. wide, interior shutters	2 pairs	$ _____
Freight			$ _____
Plumbing			
Sink	Double bowl, stainless steel	1	$ _____
Faucet	Two handle, stainless steel	1	$ _____
Plumber (labor)			$ _____
Lighting	Under-cabinet fluorescent, pendant	1 each	$ _____
Installation (labor)			$ _____

Interior Designer Compensation			$ _____
Approximate Project Cost			$ 25,000

After the preliminary budget is complete, the client has a financial setback and must reduce the amount spent on the remodel to $20,000. What suggestions can you make to reduce costs by 20 percent, or $5,000?

_____

_____

_____

_____

_____

_____

_____

Terms for the Process of Design

Name _____

Date _____   Period _____

Complete the following sentences by writing the missing word(s) in the space provided.

_____ 1. To reach a client's goals, an interior designer uses the ____ ____, a series of organized phases to carry out a project in an organized manner.

_____ 2. A ____ ____ ____ spells out the scope of project services and the responsibilities of each party, designer, and client.

_____ 3. An upfront fee the client pays to engage the services of a designer is called a(n) ____.

_____ 4. During the ____ ____, the designer identifies client objectives and requirements, gathers project information from the client, and prepares a broad concept statement to guide design.

_____ 5. A concise biographical sketch about a client is called a(n) ____.

_____ 6. A(n) ____ ____ shows the desired relationship of room and space locations.

_____ 7. A(n) ____ ____ looks at the impact of specific needs on various spaces.

_____ 8. The designer creates diagrams to develop solutions and conceptual space plans, and selects initial furniture and finishes during the ____ ____ ____.

_____ 9. Quick, freehand sketches to show space arrangements are called ____.

_____ 10. A wall covering sample large enough to show an entire pattern repeat is called a(n) ____ ____.

_____ 11. A sample to confirm the actual dye lot color is called a(n) ____ ____ ____.

_____ 12. During the ____ ____ ____, the designer creates, develops, and refines drawings and specifications based on observation, imagination, and experiences.

_____ 13. A statement that includes products, work, and fees for a project is a(n) ____.

_____ 14. A ____ ____ is a document that outlines the details of a plan change.

_____ 15. During the ____ ____ ____, the designer prepares documents that relate to interior construction.

_____ 16. During the ____ ____ ____, the designer facilitates the project by issuing bid documents and receiving proposals, purchasing products, performing site visits, and overseeing construction, holding project meetings for coordination, and executing project completion.

_____ 17. Many designers hire out, or ____, much of the work to subcontractors.

_____ 18. The interior designer serves as the ____, or connecting agent, between the client and the other persons involved in the project.

_____ 19. A ____ ____ is a document that lists unfinished tasks, missing items or damaged goods, or subpar craftsmanship that a contractor must complete prior to final payment.

Creating a Client Home Inventory

Activity A   Name_____

Chapter 18   Date_____   Period _____

Presume a family member is your new client who wants to remodel and redesign two rooms of your home. Select two rooms and complete the following chart, inserting your list of furnishings for the rooms. Use text Figure 18.1 as a guide.

Location	Description	Qty	Size	Keep	Restore	Remove	Replace	Purchase	Photo	Notes/Issues

Design Communication Terms

Activity B

Chapter 18

Name_____

Date_____   Period _____

Complete the following sentences by writing the missing word(s) in the space provided.

_____ 1. The transmission of ideas through speech is also called ____ ____.

_____ 2. The transmission of ideas through a medium that people can read is called ____ ____.

_____ 3. The transmission of ideas through a medium that people can view is called ____ ____.

_____ 4. A(n) ____ is a complete listing of property or belongings of a person or company—such as existing furniture, fixtures, or equipment—to determine what might or might not be reused.

_____ 5. Documentation proving permission has been received from a local authority to build or renovate a building is called a building ____.

_____ 6. ____ ____ is the process a project team uses to methodically utilize multiple software packages in a particular order for certain tasks to create successful, coordinated, and efficient design documents for a project.

_____ 7. A box of information that at a minimum includes the project title, author, drawing name, scale, and date is called a(n) ____ ____.

_____ 8. Perspective drawings are constructed using a(n) ____ ____, indicating the eye level of the viewer.

_____ 9. A(n) ____ ____ on a perspective drawing represents the point at which parallel lines converge.

_____ 10. The quality of two or more visual elements in a straight line or arranged in a parallel manner is called ____.

_____ 11. ____ is the nearness or closeness of two or more items or people.

_____ 12. Substances such as hot glue, rubber cement, and spray mount that stick materials together are called ____.

_____ 13. A combination of quick, small-scale sketches of the layout and components of the pages within a portfolio—typically in sequential order—is called a(n) ____.

_____ 14. The perspective distortion of a photograph, the effect by which the picture seems to get larger at the top and/or bottom is called ____.

_____ 15. During a(n) ____ ____, a designer is selling the quality of his/her future services to a potential client, clarifying experience and abilities.

_____ 16. During a(n) ____ ____, a designer's goal is to educate the client and obtain his/her approval on the design choices the designer has made.

_____ 17 A form of nonverbal communication without words that uses facial expressions and gestures is called ____ ____.

_____ 18. ____ ____ includes words that do not add depth or content to your presentations and explanations.

Example or Non-example of Effective Design Visuals

Activity C

Chapter 18

Name_____

Date_____   Period _____

Read through each of the following statements regarding the fundamentals of visual presentation materials. Based on text information, determine if each statement is an *example* or *non-example* of an effective practice for creating visual presentation materials. In the space to the left of each statement, write "E" for *example* or "N" for *non-example*.

_____ 1. Place the center of gravity on the visual slightly above center so that the visual does not feel bottom-heavy.

_____ 2. Layout of the content of the presentation chronologically left-to-right and top-down.

_____ 3. Place the title information or consistent logo at the top or top right to keep the viewer focused on the design board or web page.

_____ 4. Place an element, such as the floor plan, in the center of the composition. A layout that radiates from the center of the composition implies growth and ties all elements back to the central element.

_____ 5. Show examples of lighting higher on the board or page, and show floor patterns and coverings lower on the presentation.

_____ 6. Use limited contrast with visuals to help the viewer recognize details.

_____ 7. Dark backgrounds are best for pictures, renderings, or any materials with a pattern to enhance your visual presentation.

_____ 8. Choose only a few accent colors to use for borders and framing, and be consistent with their use.

_____ 9. To avoid confusion on the design board, use proximity to group items together. For instance, group items room by room or by product (flooring, furniture, paint, etc.).

_____ 10. Use repetition to unify your design and to give harmony and consistency to a set of design boards, portfolio pages, or web pages.

_____ 11. Whether presenting individual boards or slides in a digital presentation, use varying background colors, sizes, and orientations to keep the viewer's interest.

_____ 12. Ensure multiple complementary items are the same scale when showing then together on a board or page.

_____ 13. Use simple fonts consistently on design boards and digital presentations to successfully relay information that accompanies images.

_____ 14. Consistently use capitalization in running text with little variation in size or color.

_____ 15. Creating a grid for layout helps you effectively align the graphics and text to create strong lines and a sense of organization on boards or pages.

_____ 16. Photos and drawings are the most important elements on presentation boards and visuals. Make them the focal point of each layout and give them the majority of space.

Creating Presentation Boards

Name_____

Date_____   Period _____

An effective presentation board helps you tell the design story you desire to a client. Review the chart below. For each category in the left column, write three tips to remember for creating an effective design board in the right column. Then, respond to the items that follow the chart.

Board Categories	Tips for Creating Effective Board Design
Planning the Board	
Coding and Labeling the Board	
Mounting Floor Plans, Elevations, and Renderings	
Selecting and Mounting Samples	

1. What design strategies contribute to harmony in a design board? _____

_____

2. In your opinion, why are accuracy and precision important when creating design boards?

_____

_____

_____

Chapter 19

Textiles for Environments

Fiber Facts

Name_____

Date_____ Period _____

Select three natural fibers and seven manufactured fibers. Complete the information in the chart, listing two strengths and two weaknesses of each fiber.

	Fiber	Characteristics	
		Strengths	**Weaknesses**
Natural	1.	1. _____ 2. _____	1. _____ 2. _____
	2.	1. _____ 2. _____	1. _____ 2. _____
	3.	1. _____ 2. _____	1. _____ 2. _____
Manufactured	4.	1. _____ 2. _____	1. _____ 2. _____
	5.	1. _____ 2. _____	1. _____ 2. _____
	6.	1. _____ 2. _____	1. _____ 2. _____
	7.	1. _____ 2. _____	1. _____ 2. _____
	8.	1. _____ 2. _____	1. _____ 2. _____
	9.	1. _____ 2. _____	1. _____ 2. _____
	10.	1. _____ 2. _____	1. _____ 2. _____

Understanding Household Textiles

Activity B

Chapter 19

Name_____

Date_____   Period _____

Review the images of woven, knitted, and nonwoven fabrics. Then, answer the questions that follow each image in the space provided.

Woven Fabric

arigato/Shutterstock.com

1. How are woven fabrics made? _____

_____

2. What are warp yarns?_____

3. What are weft yarns?_____

4. List the three basic weaves. _____

5. Two variations of the plain weave are _____ .

6. Long floats (as in satin weave) tend to make a fabric less _____ than other basic weaves.

_____

7. In the _____ weave, yarn loops or cut yarns stand away from the fabric base. _____

8. Fabrics that have a _____ appear different from varying directions. _____

9. What type of weave is the example above? _____

10. List advantages of using woven fabric._____

_____

_____

_____

11. List disadvantages of using woven fabric. _____

_____

_____

_____

(Continued)

Knitted Fabric

12. How are knitted fabrics made?_____

_____

13. Why are knitted fabrics not used as often as woven fabrics in the home? _____

_____

_____

14. What is the major use of knitted fabrics in the home? _____

_____

_____

Nonwoven Fabric

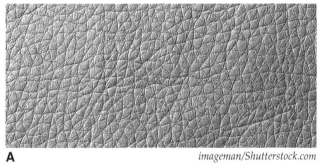

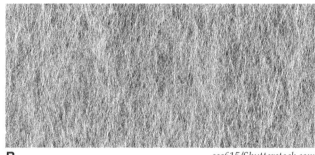

15. List the most common nonwoven fabrics used in the home. _____

_____

16. How are examples A and B above similar and different?_____

_____

17. What are the advantages of using nonwoven fabric?_____

_____

_____

18. What are the disadvantages of using nonwoven fabric?_____

_____

_____

Copyright Goodheart-Willcox Co., Inc.

May not be reproduced or posted to a publicly accessible website.

Chapter 19   *Textiles for Environments*   97

Textile Finishes

Name_____

Date_____ Period _____

Complete the following chart by summarizing the benefits of each type of textile finish in the space provided.

Basic Textile Finishes	
Type of Finish	**Benefits**
Antibacterial; antimicrobial	
Antistatic	
Bleaching	
Crease-resistant	
Durable press	
Flame-resistant; flame-retardant	
Moth resistance	
Napping	
Preshrinking	
Sizing	
Soil release	
Stain resistance (soil resistance)	
Waterproof	
Water repellent	

Choosing Textiles

When selecting fabrics for the home, several factors are important, but one may be more important than the others in a specific situation. In the chart that follows, briefly describe each factor to consider when choosing textiles for the home. Then, describe a specific situation or household item in which this factor would be the most important factor to consider.

Factor	Description	Situation/Item Most Important
Appearance		
Durability		
Maintenance		
Comfort		
Ease of Use in Construction		
Cost		

Fabrics for Window Treatments

Name_____

Date_____   Period _____

Use the Internet to locate an image of fabric that could be used for curtains or draperies. Insert the website link (URL) below the "Fabric" heading in the chart. Then, locate a photo of a window treatment appropriate for this fabric and insert the website link (URL) under the "Window Treatment" heading. (*Note:* You can also attach images of fabric and window treatments to the printed activity.) Write your answers to the questions or statements that follow in the space provided.

Fabric	Window Treatment

1. In what room would this window be located? _____

2. What function would this window treatment serve?_____

   _____

3. Describe the texture of this fabric._____

   _____

4. Describe the opaqueness of this fabric. _____

5. What is the fiber content of this fabric?_____

6. Describe durability characteristics of this fiber in terms of each of the following characteristics.

   A. sunlight resistance:_____

       _____

   B. abrasion resistance:_____

       _____

   C. cleaning process: _____

       _____

   D. other characteristics: _____

       _____

7. Why is this fabric a good choice for this particular window treatment?_____

   _____

   _____

   _____

   _____

Understanding Surface Materials and Treatments

Floor Treatments

Activity A   Name_____

Chapter 20   Date_____   Period _____

Search online for photos of floor treatments for the indicated areas and needs. Insert the website address (URL) in the space provided in the table that follows (or attach photos of floor treatments from current design magazines or online sources if using the printed activity). In the space provided, explain why each choice is appropriate for the given situation. Provide details about the cost and maintenance of each choice.

Kitchens	
Household with Preschoolers	**Household for Person Who Uses a Wheelchair**
Website address:_____ _____ Explanation: _____ _____ _____ _____ _____ _____ Cost/maintenance: _____ _____	Website address:_____ _____ Explanation: _____ _____ _____ _____ _____ _____ Cost/maintenance: _____ _____
Sleeping Area	
Nursery for Young Children	**Teens**
Website address:_____ _____ Explanation: _____ _____ _____ _____ _____ _____ Cost/maintenance: _____ _____	Website address:_____ _____ Explanation: _____ _____ _____ _____ _____ _____ Cost/maintenance: _____ _____

Estimating Carpeting and Paint

Activity B   Name_____

Chapter 20   Date _____   Period _____

Measure a living room and bedroom and record these measurements in the space that follows. Then, use the formulas provided in this activity to estimate the amounts of carpeting, ceiling paint (one coat), and wall paint (one coat) needed to design each room.

Living room (width, length, and height): _____

Bedroom (width, length, and height): _____

A—Carpeting Estimation

Step 1: Calculate area of the floor.

   Width × Length = Area

   Living room   _____ × _____ = _____ sq. ft.

   Bedroom   _____ × _____ = _____ sq. ft.

Step 2: Convert square feet into square yards.

   Area (sq. ft.) ÷ 9 = Area (sq. yd.)

   Living room   _____ ÷ 9 = _____ sq. yd.

   Bedroom   _____ ÷ 9 = _____ sq. yd.

B—Ceiling Paint Estimation

Step 1: Calculate ceiling area.

   Width × Length = Area (sq. ft.)

   Living room ceiling area   _____ × _____ = _____ sq. ft.

   Bedroom ceiling area   _____ × _____ = _____ sq. ft.

Step 2: Calculate how many gallons of paint are needed.

   Area ÷ 350 = Gallons of paint needed

   Gallons of paint needed for living room   _____ ÷ 350 = _____ (round up to the nearest gallon)

   Gallons of paint needed for bedroom   _____ ÷ 350 = _____ (round up to the nearest gallon)

(Continued)

C—Wall Paint Estimation

Step 1: Calculate the area of the four walls.

Perimeter × Height = Area

Living room walls area   _____ × _____ = _____ sq. ft.

Bedroom walls area   _____ × _____ = _____ sq. ft.

Step 2: Calculate the area of each door and window.

Width × Length = Area

Living room

Door area   _____ × _____ = _____ sq. ft.

Window area   _____ × _____ = _____ sq. ft.

Total door and window area   _____ sq. ft.

Bedroom

Door area   _____ × _____ = _____ sq. ft.

Window area   _____ × _____ = _____ sq. ft.

Total door and window area   = _____ sq. ft.

Step 3: Subtract total of door and window areas from wall area.

Living room   _____ – _____ = _____ sq. ft.

Bedroom   _____ – _____ = _____ sq. ft.

Step 4: Calculate how many gallons of paint are needed.

Area ÷ 350 = Gallons of paint needed

Gallons of paint needed for living room   _____ ÷ 350 = _____ (round up to the nearest gallon)

Gallons of paint needed for bedroom   _____ ÷ 350 = _____ (round up to the nearest gallon)

Copyright Goodheart-Willcox Co., Inc.

May not be reproduced or posted to a publicly accessible website.

Chapter 20   *Understanding Surface Materials and Treatments*   103

Terms for Surface Materials and Treatments

Name_____

Date_____   Period _____

Use the following terms to complete the sentences below. Write the missing word(s) in the space provided.

butcher block	engineered quartz	laminate	soft floor coverings
ceiling treatment	faux finish	paint	stenciling
ceramic tile	floor coverings	porcelain tile	wall covering
cork	floor treatments	resilient floor covering	wall treatments
countertop	flooring materials		

_____ 1. _____ _____ consist of flooring materials and floor coverings.

_____ 2. Materials that form the top surface of a floor are known as _____ _____.

_____ 3. A flat piece of kiln-fired clay coated with a protective glaze is called _____ _____.

_____ 4. Made of white or light clay, _____ _____ is the highest quality ceramic tile made.

_____ 5. _____ _____ are surfaces placed over the structural floor.

_____ 6. Consisting of natural and manufactured fibers, _____ _____ _____ include carpets and rugs.

_____ 7. _____ _____ _____ are floor treatments that are generally nonabsorbent, durable, easy to maintain, and fairly inexpensive.

_____ 8. Manufactured floor covering made by uniting one or more different layers, usually a decorative surface to a sturdy core, is called _____.

_____ 9. Made from the woody bark tissue of a sustainable plant, _____ has a rich appearance and is good for walking comfort.

_____ 10. A surface treatment that is applied to an interior wall is a(n) _____ _____.

_____ 11. A mixture of pigment and liquid that thinly coats and covers a surface is known as _____.

_____ 12. From the French word meaning *false*, paint professionals can achieve a(n) _____ _____ by applying paint to walls with tools other than a common paintbrush.

_____ 13. _____ is applying paint by using a cutout form to outline a design or lettering on a wall.

_____ 14. Decorative paper or vinyl applied to a wall with a special paste or adhesive is known as a(n) _____ _____.

_____ 15. A coating, covering, or building material applied to the ceiling area is called a(n) _____.

_____ 16. A durable work surface installed on a base cabinet is a(n) _____.

_____ 17. A popular type of countertop that looks like natural granite or marble is _____.

_____ 18. A work surface made by fusing together a stack of long, thin hardwood strips is called _____ _____.

Chapter 21

Furniture Styles and Window Treatments

Identifying Furniture Styles

Activity A

Chapter 21

Name _____

Date _____ Period _____

Identify each of these furniture styles and match it to its description on the next page. Then, arrange them into the three groupings by indicating the letter and the name of the style in the chart, also on the next page.

3dimentii/Shutterstock.com **A**	*sgame/Shutterstock.com* **B**	*AlexAvich/Shutterstock.com* **C**	*Mountain Light Studios/Shutterstock.com* **D**
Michael Ransburg/Shutterstock.com **E**	*Michael Ransburg/Shutterstock.com* **F**	*AlexAvich/Shutterstock.com* **G**	*Margo Harrison/Shutterstock.com* **H**
Olemac/Shutterstock.com **I**	*Arsgera/Shutterstock.com* **J**	*James Marvin/Shutterstock.com* **K**	*©iStock.com/richcat* **L**
AlexAvich/Shutterstock.com **M**	*Marko Bradic/Shutterstock.com* **N**		

(Continued)

_____ 1. Excessive use of ornamentation and massive proportions.

_____ 2. Turning and fluting on oak furniture.

_____ 3. Brass-tipped dog feet, curved legs, and rolled-top rails.

_____ 4. Dignified style made popular by Napoleon.

_____ 5. Simple, curved lines, classic motifs, and fluted columns.

_____ 6. Splat-back chairs with curved top edges.

_____ 7. Graceful lines based on flower forms; considered "new art" at the time.

_____ 8. An example of Early American furniture; usually made from maple, pine, and oak.

_____ 9. Graceful and comfortable with cabriole legs and carved fans and shells.

_____ 10. Classical and symmetrical with tapered, straight legs; named after the designers who were popular in Britain in the 1700s.

_____ 11. Delicate with curved lines, soft colors, and smaller proportions.

_____ 12. Bold, curved lines, which reflect an interest in the ancient cultures of Greece, Rome, and Egypt.

_____ 13. Cube-shaped chair with chrome frame.

_____ 14. Graceful lines; backs with shield, oval, and heart shapes.

French		English		American	
Letter	Style Name	Letter	Style Name	Letter	Style Name

Identifying Wood Joints

Name _____

Date _____   Period _____

Identify and label each of the wood joints pictured. Then, match each joint to two descriptions below.

A. _____

B. _____

C. _____

D. _____

E. _____

F. _____

_____ 1. This joint is used where several boards are joined lengthwise.

_____ 2. For this type of joint, one board is simply glued or nailed flush to another.

_____ 3. This joint has glued wooden dowels which fit into the holes drilled in both pieces of wood.

_____ 4. This joint is invisible if done skillfully.

_____ 5. This joint uses small pieces of wood attached between corner boards.

_____ 6. This is the weakest of all the wood joints.

_____ 7. This is one of the strongest joints used to join rails or legs to chairs, tables, and headboards.

_____ 8. This type of joint is used to fasten pieces of wood that meet at right angles by cutting an interlocking pattern in both pieces.

_____ 9. This type of joint is found in drawers of good-quality furniture.

_____ 10. This joint is constructed by tightly fitting a piece of wood with a notch in it to a piece of wood with a hole cut to match the notch.

_____ 11. This joint is used in chairs and tables to keep one side from pulling away from the other.

_____ 12. This joint is common and very strong.

Identifying Parts of Upholstered Furniture

Name_____

Date _____   Period _____

In the space provided, write the letter of the chair part next to its description. Then, answer the items that follow.

Calico Corners—Calico Home Stores

_____ 1. Box pleat

_____ 2. Kiln-dried hardwood frame

_____ 3. Woven fabric base

_____ 4. Loose filling

_____ 5. Coil seat springs

_____ 6. Staples

7. What is the difference between coil springs and flat springs? When might each be used in upholstered furniture?

_____

_____

_____

_____

8. What are two types of cushion filling for upholstered furniture? _____

_____

_____

_____

Choosing Window Treatments

Activity D

Chapter 21

Name _____

Date _____   Period _____

Identify a window treatment that is appropriate for each window style shown below. Write its name in the space provided. Locate an image of each treatment online and write the website link (URL) below the treatment name. (*Note:* Attach images to this worksheet if using a print copy.)

Awning

1. _____

URL: _____

Horizontal sliding

2. _____

URL: _____

Hopper

3. _____

URL: _____

Double-hung

4. _____

URL: _____

Casement

5. _____

URL: _____

Fixed

6. _____

URL: _____

Goodheart-Willcox Publisher

Measuring for Window Treatments

Name_____

Date _____ Period _____

In the space provided, describe in your own words how to measure windows for draperies, curtains, and cafe curtains. Use labels wherever they make your descriptions clearer.

Draperies

_____
_____
_____
_____
_____
_____

Curtains

_____
_____
_____
_____
_____

Cafe Curtains

Goodheart-Willcox Publisher

Selection of Furnishings, Accessories, and Art

Planning for Furnishings and Accessories

Activity A   Name_____

Chapter 22   Date _____   Period _____

Presume you are a housing and interior design professional who is helping a new client select furnishings and accessories, and plan a preliminary budget for his great room furniture. Your client has up to $5000.00 to spend on the great room and likes modern furniture with ergonomics as a priority. He uses the room for entertaining, relaxing, and watching movies. Review the following great room floor plan, noting the entrances and fireplace that influence furniture selection and placement. Use online resources to select furnishings and accessories for your client's room, including quantity, style/color, and estimated cost of items. Then, complete the preliminary furnishings and accessories budget that follows. List the website link (URL) in the "Item/Product" column for your choices.

Evita Van Zoeren/Shutterstock.com

Preliminary Furnishings and Accessories Plan and Budget			
Item/Product/URL	Quantity	Style/Color	Estimated Cost

Total estimated cost of furnishings and accessories:_____

Deciding Where to Shop for Furniture

Activity B

Name_____

Chapter 22

Date _____ Period _____

Using online resources, visit four different sites of retailers that sell furniture. Include sites for a major department store, a warehouse showroom, and an Internet-based business. List each retailer's name, the type of retailer it is, and the website link (URL). Then, list the services available at each, and compare the prices and quality of similar items.

Retailer 1

Name:_____ Type: _____

URL: _____

Services available:_____

_____

Prices of furniture: _____

Quality of furniture: _____

Retailer 2

Name:_____ Type: _____

URL: _____

Services available:_____

_____

Prices of furniture: _____

Quality of furniture: _____

Retailer 3

Name:_____ Type: _____

URL: _____

Services available:_____

_____

Prices of furniture: _____

Quality of furniture: _____

Retailer 4

Name:_____ Type: _____

URL: _____

Services available:_____

_____

Prices of furniture: _____

Quality of furniture: _____

Where would you prefer to purchase furniture? Explain. _____

_____

Using Accessories

Name_____

Date_____   Period _____

Use online resources to locate an image of a room that you think shows effective use of furniture and accessories in the room. In the space provided, write the website link (URL) of a picture showing good use of accessories in a room and briefly describe the room and its furnishings (or if using a print copy, attach a copy of the image). In the chart below, list each accessory in the appropriate column, and answer the question following the chart.

URL: _____

Description: _____

_____

_____

_____

_____

Functional Accessories	Decorative Accessories	Dual-Purpose Accessories

Considering color, style, and purpose, how do these accessories tie the room's furnishings together?

_____

_____

_____

_____

_____

Selecting and Placing Art

Activity D   Name_____

Chapter 22   Date_____   Period _____

Presume your new client has hired you to select and place art on the sofa wall of the living room. Examine the photo of the room below. Your client's walls are gray, the sofa is white, and the hardwood floor has a gray tint. Your client is a single female who uses the room for entertaining, relaxing, and reading. After analyzing the image, use online resources to search for three art examples you might suggest to your client. Complete the chart below, writing the website links (URLs) for your selections in the space provided. Also include details about each design element, including scale, shape and orientation, contrast, height, and balance of the art with the wall, sofa, and accessories.

Markus Gann/Shutterstock.com

Design Elements	Art Example 1/URL	Art Example 2/URL	Art Example 3/URL
Scale and Size What scale is each item or group of items in relation to the wall and sofa?			
Shape and Orientation How do the shape and orientation of the item or group of items fit the space?			
Contrast How do the items add contrast to the space?			
Height Does the height of the items provide a focal point at eye level? How?			
Balance Do the items provide formal or informal balance?			

Acquiring Housing

Evaluating a Place to Rent

Activity A   Name_____

Chapter 23   Date_____   Period _____

Part 1: Make an appointment to see or visit an apartment that is open to the public and complete the *Apartment Renters' Checklist*. (Some virtual tours of apartments are available online.) Place a check mark (✓) beside each item the apartment meets.

Apartment Renters' Checklist

Laundry Facilities

_____ How many washers and dryers are available? (A good ratio is one washer and dryer for every 10 apartments.)

_____ Are washers and dryers in good working order?

Building Lobby

_____ Is the lobby clean and well lit?

_____ Is the main entrance locked so only residents can enter?

_____ Is a security guard provided? If so, during what hours?

Entrance, Exit, and Halls

_____ Are elevators provided? If so, are they in good working order?

_____ Are the stairs soundly constructed and well lit?

_____ Are fire exits provided?

_____ Is there a fire alarm or other warning system?

_____ Are halls clean, well lit, and soundly constructed?

Bathroom(s)

_____ Do all plumbing fixtures work? Are they clean?

_____ Does the hot water supply seem adequate?

_____ Do floors and walls around fixtures seem damp, rotted, or moldy?

Kitchen

_____ Is the sink working and clean? Does it have drain stoppers?

_____ Is there an exhaust fan above the range?

(Continued)

_____ Is the refrigerator working properly? Does it have a separate freezer compartment?

_____ If there is a dishwasher, does it work properly?

Air Conditioning and Heating

_____ Is the building centrally air conditioned or are there separate units in each apartment?

_____ Does the air conditioning unit work properly?

_____ What type of heat is provided (gas, electric)?

_____ Does the heating system work properly?

_____ Is there a fireplace? If so, are there smoke stains or other signs that it has not worked properly?

_____ Are there smoke detectors and carbon monoxide detectors located in each apartment as identified by local and state law?

Wiring

_____ Are there enough electrical outlets? (There should be at least three to a room.)

_____ Do all switches and outlets work?

_____ Are there enough circuits in the fuse box or circuit breaker panel to handle all your electrical equipment?

Lighting

_____ Are there enough fixtures for adequate light? Are the fixtures in good working order?

_____ Does the apartment get a good amount of natural light from windows?

Windows

_____ Are any windows broken or difficult to open and close?

_____ Are windows arranged to provide good ventilation?

_____ Are screens provided?

_____ Are there drafts around the window frame?

_____ In high-rise buildings, does the landlord arrange for the outside of the windows to be cleaned? If so, how often?

Floors

_____ Are floors clean and free of gouges?

_____ Do floors have any water stains indicating previous leaks?

Ceilings

_____ Are ceilings clean and free of cracks and peeling?

_____ Are there any water stains indicating previous leaks?

(Continued)

Walls

_____ Are walls clean and free of cracks and peeling?

_____ Does the paint run or smear when rubbed with a damp cloth?

Soundproofing

_____ When you thump the walls, do they seem hollow or solid?

_____ Can you hear neighbors downstairs, upstairs, or on either side of you?

Telephone, Television, and Internet

_____ Are phone jacks already installed?

_____ Are phone jacks in convenient locations?

_____ Is an outside antenna connection provided?

_____ Is a cable TV connection provided?

_____ Are connections for Internet service available?

Storage Space

_____ Is there adequate closet space?

_____ Are there enough kitchen and bathroom cabinets?

_____ Is additional storage space provided for tenants?

Outdoor Play Space

_____ Are outdoor facilities provided? If so, are the facilities well maintained?

Part 2: Interview the landlord and record his or her comments using the questions that follow.

1. What is the rent per month? How and when must it be paid?_____

_____

2. Is a security deposit required? If so, how much is it? Under what conditions will it be returned?

_____

_____

_____

3. Does the lease say that rent can be increased if real estate or other expenses to the landlord are raised?

_____

_____

_____

(Continued)

4. What expenses are there in addition to rent? (These may include utilities, storage space, air conditioning, parking space, master TV antenna or cable TV connections, use of a pool or other recreational areas, installation of special appliances, and late payment of rent.)

_____

_____

_____

5. How are deliveries of packages handled? _____

_____

6. Is loud noise prohibited at certain hours? _____

7. How are Internet connections provided?_____

Part 3: Evaluate the apartment using the following statement and questions. Write a summary about your thoughts in the space provided.

Describe your overall impression of this apartment.

_____

_____

_____

_____

_____

_____

_____

_____

_____

_____

Based on your completed evaluation, would you like to live in this apartment? Why?

_____

_____

_____

_____

_____

_____

_____

_____

_____

Understanding the Written Lease

Activity B   Name_____

Chapter 23   Date_____   Period _____

Obtain a basic lease or rental agreement online from a reputable, free source. Write the website link (URL) for the lease in the space provided and print a copy for your reference. Imagine you have signed the lease. Review the lease for answers to the following questions.

URL for written lease:_____

1. According to the lease, what might happen if you damage the landlord's property?_____

_____

_____

2. What is the landlord required to provide if your security deposit is withheld because of damage to the apartment?

_____

_____

_____

3. You decide to move when your lease expires. In what condition must you leave the apartment when you move?

_____

_____

4. The roof leaks and damages your television. Is the landlord responsible for the damage to your television?

_____

_____

5. If you find that paying the rent and other expenses is more difficult than you had expected, does the lease allow you to get a roommate to move in and share expenses with you?

_____

_____

6. Can you paint or apply wall covering to the walls and hang pictures on the walls?_____

7. Can you install partitions in your living room? _____

8. Can you install new locks on the doors? _____

9. Can you place campaign signs in your windows?_____

10. Are you allowed to have a waterbed? _____

11. Can you have a piano and give piano lessons in your apartment? _____

(Continued)

12. Are you allowed to have a grill on the balcony? _____

13. Are you allowed to keep a dog or other pet in the apartment? _____

14. When and under what circumstances must you allow your landlord free access to your apartment?

_____

_____

_____

_____

_____

_____

15. If your bicycle is stolen from the storage room, is your landlord liable? _____

16. Under the terms of the lease, what are the possible consequences if you move out before the lease expires?

_____

_____

_____

_____

_____

_____

17. Under the terms of the lease, what are the possible consequences if you fail to pay your rent?

_____

_____

_____

_____

_____

_____

18. Under the terms of the lease, what are the possible consequences if you fail to comply with the terms of the lease?

_____

_____

_____

_____

_____

_____

Real Estate Research

Name_____

Date_____ Period _____

Use reliable online resources—such as websites for the *Occupational Outlook Handbook (OOH), O*NET,* the *National Association of Realtors,* and the *National Association of Real Estate Brokers*—to answer the following questions about real estate agents or brokers. Then, visit the website of a local real estate firm to find out about the availability of housing in your community.

List the responsibilities of a real estate agent or broker. _____

_____

_____

_____

_____

What training and other qualifications are required to become a real estate agent or broker?

_____

_____

What is the future employment outlook for a real estate agent or broker? _____

_____

When should someone seek the services of a real estate agent or broker?_____

_____

_____

_____

Once a buyer finds a house, how long does it usually take to settle legal and financial matters so the buyer can move in?

_____

_____

_____

List and visit the website of a real estate firm in your area.

_____

_____

According to the website, list types of real estate available in your community.

_____

_____

_____

Meeting Financial Guidelines—Buying a House

Name_____

Date_____   Period _____

Read the following paragraph about a young couple who are planning to buy a house. Calculate their *housing-to-income ratio* and their *debt-to-income ratio*. Then, answer the questions that follow.

> Rita and Josh Carter want to buy a house. They have an annual combined income of $87,000 with gross monthly pay of $7,250. The potential house payment is $925 monthly. Other monthly housing-related costs total $800—which covers property taxes, home owner's insurance, utilities, repairs, and maintenance. They owe $825 monthly on long-term debts (those taking over 10 months to pay) for two car loans, college education costs, and an entertainment system. Would the Carters meet approval guidelines to obtain a loan for the house?

To answer this question, the Carters must meet two ratios. They include

Housing-to-Income Ratio (must be 28% or less)	Debt-to-Income Ratio (must be 36% or less)
To calculate the housing-to-income ratio, use the following formula: (Show your work in the space provided.) Total Housing Costs ÷ Gross Income = (result) × 100 = Housing-to-Income Ratio	To calculate the debt-to-income ratio, first add together the total housing costs and long-term debt. Then, use the following formula: (Show your work in the space provided.) Total Debt ÷ Gross Income = (result) × 100 = Debt-to-Income Ratio
Your calculations:	Your calculations:

1. What is the Carters' housing-to-income ratio? _____

2. Do the Carters meet this guideline? _____

3. What is the Carters' debt-to-income ratio? _____

4. Do the Carters meet this guideline? _____

5. In addition to these guidelines, what else might affect the Carters in getting approval for a home loan?

The Details of Acquiring Housing

Activity E

Chapter 23

Name_____

Date_____ Period _____

Complete the following sentences by writing the missing word(s) in the space provided before each number.

_____ 1. A partial payment made to secure a purchase is a(n) ____ ____.

_____ 2. The price paid for the use of someone else's money is known as ____.

_____ 3. The process of buying something by making a series of payments during a given length of time is called ____ ____.

_____ 4. The extra amount charged for using credit that includes interest and other service fees is the ____ ____.

_____ 5. A payment that insures the building owner against financial loss caused by the renter is called a(n) ____ ____.

_____ 6. A(n) ____ is a legal document spelling out the conditions of the rental agreement.

_____ 7. A property owner (landlord) is known as the ____.

_____ 8. A renter is known as the ____.

_____ 9. The transfer of part interest of a rental property to someone else is to ____, which means that both parties are responsible to the landlord for all terms of the lease.

_____ 10. Failure to meet all terms of a contract or agreement is known as ____ ____ ____.

_____ 11. ____ is a legal procedure that forces a renter to leave the property before the rental agreement expires.

_____ 12. The original sum borrowed for the purchase of a home is called the ____.

_____ 13. The money value of a house beyond what is owed on it is the ____.

_____ 14. A legal proceeding in which a lending firm takes possession of the property when the owner fails to make monthly house payments ____.

_____ 15. Income before deductions is called ____ ____.

_____ 16. The division of total housing costs by gross income is the ____-____-____ ____.

_____ 17. The division of total debt (debt + housing costs) by gross income is the ____-____-____ ____.

_____ 18. A profile of a person's payment record and outstanding debts is the ____ ____.

(Continued)

_____ 19. A fee contractors charge to build a house, which includes both materials and labor costs, is called a(n) _____.

_____ 20. A pledge of property that a borrower gives to a lender as security for a loan with which to buy the property is called a(n) _____.

_____ 21. To pay off a loan (principal with interest) in monthly installments for a given number of years is to _____.

_____ 22. A two-party contract between a borrower and lender, which is a loan with a long-term fixed rate, is a(n) _____ _____.

_____ 23. A mortgage for which the interest rate is periodically adjusted up or down according to a national interest rate index is a(n) _____ _____ _____.

_____ 24. A three-party contract that involves the borrower, a lender, and the Federal Housing Administration (FHA) is a(n) _____ - _____ _____.

_____ 25. A three-party contract that involves the borrower (who is a veteran of the U.S. Armed Forces), a lending firm, and the Veterans Administration (VA) is a(n) _____ - _____ _____.

_____ 26. A deposit, or sum of money, a home buyer pays to show serious intentions to buy a house is called _____ _____.

_____ 27. A document that gives a detailed description of the property and its legal location and all specific terms and conditions of the real estate sale is a(n) _____ _____ _____.

_____ 28. An evaluation of construction and present condition of a house, which can reveal any defects that may impact home value and sales price, is called a(n) _____ _____.

_____ 29. An expert estimate of the quality and value of a property by a licensed appraiser is a(n) _____.

_____ 30. A document that gives proof of the rights of ownership and possession of particular property is the _____.

_____ 31. The legal document that shows the transfer of title from one person to another is the _____.

_____ 32. Fees and charges for settling the legal and financial matters for a real estate sale are the _____ _____.

Home Safety and Security

Identifying Accident Causes—Taking Preventive Measures

Activity A

Chapter 24

Name_____

Date _____ Period _____

Read about the accidents listed in the chart below. List probable causes of the accidents and identify safety measures that might have prevented the accidents. Compare and discuss your responses in class.

Accident	Probable Causes	Preventive Safety Measures
1. Cora fell on the front porch.		
2. Marcus got burns on his hands when he removed a hot cookie sheet from the oven using a damp dishcloth.		
3. John got a shock when he unplugged the toaster with wet hands.		
4. Taylor's cat became very ill after eating some leaves from a new houseplant.		
5. Two-year-old Mateo swallowed an oven cleaning product stored under the kitchen sink.		
6. Three-year-old Isabelle fell into the swimming pool trying to retrieve a ball.		

Comparing Smoke Detectors and Carbon Monoxide Detectors

Activity B   Name_____

Chapter 24   Date_____   Period _____

Part 1: Use online resources to compare two types of smoke detectors. Write the information you locate in the space provided.

	Brand 1: _____ URL: _____	Brand 2: _____ URL: _____
Cost		
Warranty Information		
Operation		
Special Features (such as fire/carbon monoxide detector combination)		

Which smoke detector would you buy? Explain. _____

_____

_____

_____

_____

List where you would place smoke detectors in a dwelling. Explain. _____

_____

_____

_____

_____

(Continued)

Name_____

Part 2: Use online resources to compare two types of carbon monoxide detectors. Write the information you locate in the space provided.

	Brand 1: _____ URL: _____	Brand 2: _____ URL: _____
Cost		
Warranty Information		
Operation		
Special Features		

Which carbon monoxide detector would you buy? Explain. _____

_____

_____

_____

_____

List where you would place carbon monoxide detectors in a dwelling. Explain. _____

_____

_____

_____

_____

_____

Home Security Inspection Checklist

Activity C

Chapter 24

Name_____

Date_____   Period _____

Part 1: Conduct a home security inspection using the following checklist. Note specific issues on the checklist if you identify a problem.

✓	Entrances	Issues
	Are the doors solid wood construction or metal with secure locks?	
	Are the door frames strong enough to prevent forced entry?	
	Does each entrance have a screen or storm door with a secure lock?	
	Are all entrances well lighted?	
	Is there an automatic system that lights exterior doors from dusk to dawn or motion-detecting lights?	
	Can the entrances be observed from the street?	
	Are all entrances free from concealing landscaping (trees and shrubs)?	
	Is there an electronic security system? Does the system use biometric data?	
	Do the entrances have peepholes or chain locks to permit you to see who is at the door?	
	Do sliding glass doors have extra security devices?	
✓	**Windows**	**Issues**
	Do all windows have secure locks in working condition?	
	Do windows have screens or storm windows that lock from the inside?	
	Are window areas well lighted and free from concealing landscaping?	
✓	**Garage Doors and Windows**	**Issues**
	Is the overhead door equipped with a secure lock? Is the entry door kept closed and locked at all times?	
	If available, is the garage door opener working properly and locked when closed? Is key entry available in the event of a power outage?	
	Are tools and ladders stored in the garage, not outside?	
	Are all doors well lighted on the outside?	

(Continued)

✓	**Other Security Precautions**	**Issues**
	Do you leave a vehicle in the driveway when you are away from home?	
	Do you keep newspapers picked up each day from around the house?	
	Do you remove emptied trash cans from the curb right away?	
	Do you empty your mailbox daily or have your mail held at the post office when on vacation?	
	Do you have a variable timer to turn lights, a radio, or a TV on and off inside the house automatically?	
	Do you keep your yard mowed and snow removed from walkways, even when away from home?	
	Do you open window treatments (shades, blinds, curtains, or draperies) during the day and close them at night?	

Part 2: Review this checklist with the members of your household. Complete the chart that follows, identifying at least five security precautions you could take to improve your home security.

Security Issue	**Precautions to Improve Security**
1.	
2.	
3.	
4.	
5.	
6.	

Creating a Plan for Emergencies

Name_____

Date_____ Period _____

With the other members of your household, decide on an escape plan in case a fire or other emergency occurs. In the space provided, describe your escape plan, identifying efficient ways to escape from each floor and room of your house or apartment. List the location of exits. Then, answer the questions that follow.

Escape plan description: _____

_____

_____

_____

_____

_____

1. What signal, such as a loud whistle or a bell, will you use to communicate a fire or other emergency?

_____

2. Where will everyone meet after you exit the house or dwelling?_____

_____

3. Does everyone know how to do the *door test*? Explain how it is done. _____

_____

_____

4. Who will assist small children or older adults who might need assistance? _____

_____

5. What number do you call to reach the fire department or emergency assistance in your community?

_____

6. If your home has a second floor, do all members know where the escape ladder is located and understand how to use it?

_____

7. Do you have an emergency preparedness kit located by an exit? Do all household members know the location?

_____

8. What additional practices should you follow in a fire or other emergency? _____

_____

_____

Maintaining a Home

Analyzing Cleaning Tasks

Activity A   Name_____

Chapter 25   Date_____   Period _____

Analyze the list below by thinking about how you would handle cleaning tasks in your own home. Identify whether the cleaning activity should be accomplished daily (**D**), weekly (**W**), monthly (**M**), semiannually (**S**), annually (**A**), or never (**N**). Write your response beside each number. Compare your responses with the class.

_____ 1. Change bed linens.

_____ 2. Wash dishes.

_____ 3. Vacuum upholstered furniture and drapes, and wipe blinds.

_____ 4. Vacuum carpet.

_____ 5. Sweep kitchen floor.

_____ 6. Wash kitchen floor.

_____ 7. Wash windows.

_____ 8. Clean drapes, blinds, and other window coverings.

_____ 9. Make bed.

_____ 10. Vacuum and turn mattress; wash mattress pad.

_____ 11. Dust and polish furniture.

_____ 12. Wash or dry-clean bedding.

_____ 13. Wash or change the liner of the kitchen trash container.

_____ 14. Polish silverware.

_____ 15. Shine mirrors.

_____ 16. Wash bathroom floor.

_____ 17. Clean and organize kitchen shelves.

_____ 18. Clean closets.

_____ 19. Wipe kitchen counter and cooking surfaces; clean sink.

_____ 20. Clean refrigerator and freezer, and defrost if needed.

_____ 21. Put away clutter.

_____ 22. Remove fingerprints and marks on walls.

_____ 23. Sweep or vacuum entryways.

_____ 24. Clean bathroom sink, tub, and toilet.

_____ 25. Wash bathroom walls.

_____ 26. Wash throw rugs.

_____ 27. Tidy the bedroom, bathroom, living, and eating areas.

_____ 28. Wash seldom-used glasses and dinnerware.

_____ 29. Clean range, including oven.

_____ 30. Empty wastebaskets and other trash containers.

Assembling a Home Repair Kit

Name_____

Date_____   Period _____

Search online to itemize the cost of assembling a home repair kit. Plan a basic kit by listing in the following table the name of each item, its main use, and its cost. Then, use the text or search online to research and answer the questions that follow.

Item/Tool	Use	Cost
	Total Cost:	

1. How should a nail or screw be placed in a wall to hang a picture?_____

_____

_____

2. How should you anchor a bookcase, range, or television to a wall to prevent it from tipping over?

_____

_____

3. When an overload occurs, what procedures and precautions should you follow to restore a circuit breaker or replace a fuse?

_____

_____

_____

Meeting Storage Needs

Activity C   Name_____

Chapter 25   Date_____   Period _____

Suppose you are a professional organizer. You are working with the Johanson family—Janell and Chad Johanson who have two children, Scott, age 9, and Anastasia, age 2. Janell likes to do scrapbooking, play golf, and do photography. Chad also plays golf and loves to go fishing and do woodworking. Scott likes to ride his bike and plays a variety of sports as well as video games. Anastasia has lots of toys, as well as a stroller. The Johansons have a three-bedroom home, with a storage closet in the hallway. They also have a garage and a basement. The family has come to you to solve their storage problems. After analyzing what storage problems the Johansons might have, answer the questions that follow. Research storage items online that you might recommend to the Johansons, listing the website link (URL) for each item and a brief description.

1. Description of storage problem the Johansons might have: _____

   _____

   _____

   _____

   _____

   _____

2. Describe how you would solve this storage problem. _____

   _____

   _____

   _____

   _____

   _____

3. What storage devices would you use, if any? Describe and list the URLs for these devices, if possible.

   _____

   _____

   _____

   _____

   _____

4. What is the approximate cost of these devices? _____

5. Does your plan require any construction skills? If so, describe. _____

   _____

   _____

   _____

Redesign Recommendations

Name_____

Date_____ Period _____

Search online for a photo of an attractive room. Write the website link (URL) in the space provided with a brief description of the room (or print and attach the photo if using the print activity). Then, write your recommendations for the room design in the table below.

Photo URL: _____

Description: _____

_____

_____

_____

_____

_____

_____

Recommendations for Redesigning with a $750 Budget	Recommendations for Redesigning with a $2,000 Budget

Chapter 26
Career Planning

Identifying Career Interests

Activity A Name _____

Chapter 26 Date _____ Period _____

Answer the following questions about factors that relate to your career interests.

1. What kinds of hobbies, activities, or clubs do you enjoy? _____

_____

2. How would you rate yourself (good, fair, poor) in the following areas?

Mathematics: _____

Science: _____

Art: _____

Career and Technical Education classes (specify which): _____

_____

_____

3. Do you prefer heavy physical activity, light physical activity, or desk work? _____

_____

4. Do you like to work with equipment and build things? _____

_____

5. Are you willing to continue your education after high school? _____

What type of continuing education program (technical school, apprenticeship program, two-year college, four-year college, etc.) most interests you? _____

_____

6. Do you enjoy being outdoors or would you rather work inside? _____

7. Do you prefer to work regular hours or have a varied schedule? _____

8. Do you prefer to work with a group of coworkers, with one or two people, or alone? _____

_____

9. Do you prefer to lead a group or be a group member? _____

10. Using your answers to the above questions as a guideline, name a housing or interior design career that appeals to you. Give reasons for your choice.

_____

_____

_____

Copyright Goodheart-Willcox Co., Inc.
May not be reproduced or posted to a publicly accessible website.

Chapter 26 *Career Planning* 135

Researching Job Requirements

Name_____

Date_____   Period _____

Search job ads online for two housing- or interior design-related occupations. Write the website link (URL) for each ad in the space provided in the following chart. Then, complete the chart by inserting the details about each position.

Advertisement 1	Advertisement 2
URL: _____ _____ _____	URL: _____ _____ _____
Job title: _____ List required education, training, and experience: _____ _____ _____ _____ _____ _____ Other requirements:_____ What would you need to do to qualify for the job? _____ _____ _____ _____ _____ _____	Job title: _____ List required education, training, and experience: _____ _____ _____ _____ _____ _____ Other requirements:_____ What would you need to do to qualify for the job? _____ _____ _____ _____ _____ _____

Evaluating a Postsecondary Program

Activity C

Name_____

Chapter 26

Date_____   Period _____

Presume you have decided on a career in a housing or interior design profession. Use online resources to research postsecondary programs in your state or other state for factors essential to choosing an institution of higher education that fits your personal and career needs. Complete the following chart noting program details about your institution of choice.

Name of postsecondary institution: _____

URL for postsecondary institution: _____

Factors to Consider	Postsecondary Institution/Program Details
Accreditation	
Reputation	
Curriculum	
Program Focus	
Course Progression	
Experiences & Internships	
Student-Instructor Ratio	
Instructors	
Facility & Campus	
Industry Involvement	
Location	
Campus Life	
Personal Fit	

Navigating the Career Clusters

Activity D   Name_____

Chapter 26   Date_____   Period _____

The career clusters can help you find a career and/or an occupation you may be interested in pursuing. They can help you identify the knowledge and skills you will need. Practice using career clusters resources by answering the following questions about one of the 16 clusters, the *Architecture and Construction* cluster. Use the Advance CTE website and/or O*NET to locate information about the career clusters.

Identifying Pathways and Occupations

Each career cluster is divided into a number of career pathways. Each career pathway contains a number of occupations. In the spaces provided, write the names of the career pathways in the *Architecture and Construction* cluster. Then, choose and write the titles of three occupations included in each pathway.

Pathway:_____

    Occupation: _____

    Occupation: _____

    Occupation: _____

Pathway:_____

    Occupation: _____

    Occupation: _____

    Occupation: _____

Pathway:_____

    Occupation: _____

    Occupation: _____

    Occupation: _____

Identifying Knowledge and Skills

What knowledge and skills are necessary for careers in all clusters and pathways? These are called *Essential Knowledge and Skills*. For example: ESS01.02.03, "Organize oral and written information." Choose and list 10 others.

1. _____   6. _____

2. _____   7. _____

3. _____   8. _____

4. _____   9. _____

5. _____   10. _____

(Continued)

What knowledge and skills are necessary for all careers in the *Architecture and Construction* cluster? These are called *Cluster (Foundation) Knowledge and Skills*. For example: ACC01.01.01, "Use basic math functions to complete jobsite/workplace tasks." Choose and list 10 others.

1. _____   6. _____

2. _____   7. _____

3. _____   8. _____

4. _____   9. _____

5. _____   10. _____

What knowledge and skills are necessary for each pathway in the *Architecture and Construction* cluster? These are called *Pathway Knowledge and Skills*. For example: ESS03.01.01, "Identify common tasks that require employees to use problem-solving skills." Choose and list 5 others for each pathway.

Pathway:_____

1. _____

2. _____

3. _____

4. _____

5. _____

Pathway:_____

1. _____

2. _____

3. _____

4. _____

5. _____

Pathway:_____

1. _____

2. _____

3. _____

4. _____

5. _____

Identifying Career Terms

Activity E   Name_____

Chapter 26   Date_____   Period _____

Complete the following sentences by writing the missing word(s) in the space provided.

_____ 1. A _____ is a series of related occupations that show progression in a field of work.

_____ 2. Paid employment that involves handling one or more jobs is called a(n) _____.

_____ 3. An ability to learn something quickly and easily is a natural talent or _____.

_____ 4. Skills you develop with practice are called _____.

_____ 5. An interior designer who finalized all design decisions on a project is called a _____.

_____ 6. Workers who fill entry-level jobs that require almost no previous knowledge or experience are called _____.

_____ 7. Workers who have some experience and/or technical training are _____ _____.

_____ 8. Workers who have successfully completed a formal training program beyond high school are known as _____ _____.

_____ 9. The process of observing a person in the workplace to learn more about his/her job and its requirements is known as _____ _____.

_____ 10. A _____ is someone with greater experience and knowledge who guides you in your career.

_____ 11. An arrangement with an educational institution whereby a student is supervised while working with a more experienced jobholder within a profession is known as a(n) _____.

_____ 12. On-the-job training and classroom instruction to learn a trade under the guidance of an expert trade professional is known as a(n) _____.

_____ 13. Programs that offer opportunities to work part-time and attend classes part-time as a high school student are known as _____ _____.

_____ 14. A document that verifies completion of coursework or a program is a _____.

_____ 15. A _____ certifies that an individual has undergone the proper training to perform a profession.

_____ 16. After successfully completing a two-year college program, an individual typically earns a(n) _____ _____.

_____ 17. A _____ _____ is typically achieved after four or five years from a college or university.

_____ 18. An advanced degree from a college or university is a(n) _____ _____.

_____ 19. Groups of occupations or career specialties that are similar or related to one another are known as _____ _____.

_____ 20. The exchange of information or services among individuals or groups is known as _____.

Chapter 27

Preparing for Career Success

Online Résumés and Personal Information

Activity A

Name_____

Chapter 27

Date _____   Period _____

Study the personal information provided in the sample résumés below. Assume that the information is correct. What should be changed by the job seeker before he or she posts the résumé to an online job board? Describe what you would change and why in the space provided.

Résumé #1
Lamar Takahashi
5678 C Ave.
City, State 98765
Partyboy@Internetprovider.net
Best hours to reach me: 6–9 p.m.

Résumé #2
Olivia "The Brain" Polnachek
P.O. Box 123
City, State 98765
(111) 555-1234 home   (111) 555-5678 cell
No e-mail address provided
SSN: 555-55-5555

_____   _____

_____   _____

_____   _____

_____   _____

_____   _____

_____   _____

_____   _____

_____   _____

_____   _____

_____   _____

_____   _____

_____   _____

_____   _____

_____   _____

Planning Your Résumé

Activity B

Name_____

Chapter 27

Date_____   Period _____

Complete the following planning guide to help prepare your résumé. Follow the example on text page 640. Then, use word processing software to prepare your résumé file as directed by your instructor.

1. Personal contact information: _____

_____

_____

_____

_____

2. Employment objective:_____

_____

_____

_____

_____

3. Education: _____

_____

_____

_____

_____

_____

_____

_____

_____

4. Skills and abilities: _____

_____

_____

_____

_____

_____

_____

_____

_____

(Continued)

5. Work experience (include dates and city and state):_____

_____

_____

_____

_____

_____

_____

_____

6. Honors and activities (include name of organization or honor, dates, and city and state): _____

_____

_____

_____

_____

7. Community service:_____

_____

_____

_____

_____

8. Interests: _____

_____

_____

_____

_____

9. References (name, address, phone; acquire permission to use names): _____

_____

_____

_____

_____

_____

_____

_____

_____

Writing a Cover Message

Name_____

Date_____   Period _____

An effective cover message is your first introduction to a potential employer. It is your chance to make a positive impression. Use online resources to choose a job in which you are interested. Write the website link (URL) in the space provided. Then, write a cover message to the employer showing your interest and why you are qualified for the job. See the sample on text page 644. Remember, a cover message should be brief and to the point and include the following:

- title of the job you seek
- where or how you heard about the job
- your strengths, skills, and abilities for the job

- reasons you should be considered for the job
- when you are available to begin work
- request for an interview

Dear _____:

_____

_____

_____

_____

_____

_____

_____

_____

_____

_____

_____

_____

_____

_____

_____

_____

_____

Sincerely,

Name:_____

Address: _____

_____

Phone: _____

E-mail: _____

The Job Search

Name_____

Date_____   Period _____

Interview an adult about his or her job search experience. Record his or her responses to the questions that follow.

1. Which of the following sources did you use to find job leads? (Check all that apply.)

   _____ A. school placement office

   _____ B. online job postings

   _____ C. social networking sites

   _____ D. newspaper want ads

   _____ E. job fairs

   _____ F. professional or occupational organizations

   _____ G. family members and friends

   _____ H. other _____

   _____

2. Which of the above sources did you find most helpful? Explain your answer. _____

   _____

3. Which of the above sources did you find least helpful? Explain your answer._____

   _____

4. How have you used networking in your career? _____

   _____

5. What advice would you give someone about preparing a résumé? _____

   _____

6. What kinds of people did you use as references when searching for a job? Explain why you chose each of these people.

   _____

   _____

7. Do you have a professional portfolio?_____

   If so, what types of items have you included in it? _____

   _____

8. How did you initially contact your place of employment?

   _____ A. phone   _____ C. mail   _____ E. in person

   _____ B. fax   _____ D. e-mail

9. Did you have to complete a job application form before being interviewed for your job?_____

   If so, what, if anything, was unusual about the application form? _____

   _____

(Continued)

10. How many interviews did you have at your place of employment? _____

11. Who conducted each interview? _____

_____

12. What did you know about your place of employment before the interview?_____

_____

13. What questions did you have for the interviewer? _____

_____

14. How did you dress for the interview?_____

_____

15. What, if any, employment tests did you have to take before being hired? _____

_____

16. Did you send a follow-up letter thanking the employer for the interview?_____

17. What advice would you give someone preparing for a job interview? _____

_____

18. How many job offers did you have to consider? _____

19. How important was each of the following factors in helping you decide whether to accept the job offer you chose? (Circle the appropriate response for each factor.)

    A. physical surroundings

very important	somewhat important	neither important nor unimportant	somewhat unimportant	very unimportant

    B. work schedule

very important	somewhat important	neither important nor unimportant	somewhat unimportant	very unimportant

    C. income and benefits

very important	somewhat important	neither important nor unimportant	somewhat unimportant	very unimportant

    D. job obligations

very important	somewhat important	neither important nor unimportant	somewhat unimportant	very unimportant

    E. advancement potential

very important	somewhat important	neither important nor unimportant	somewhat unimportant	very unimportant

20. How long is your daily commute in terms of time and distance? _____

_____

Leadership as a Job Qualification

Activity E

Chapter 27

Name_____

Date_____   Period _____

Leadership skills are needed in all careers. Explain how you would handle the following situations if you were the leader.

Situation #1

You are the architect who is overseeing construction of a new house. You promised your clients their house would be ready in April. Simon, the contractor you hired to supervise construction of the house, is two months behind schedule. When you ask him why, he explains he is having trouble getting some of the specified building materials because of a truckers' strike. The homeowners do not want a substitution in materials, yet their apartment lease expires in April.

What should you do next? _____

_____

What options can you suggest? _____

_____

_____

Choose one possible option and explain how you would implement it. _____

_____

_____

_____

_____

Situation #2

You are leading a team of interior designers consisting of Sergio, Bridgette, and yourself. Your goal is to decorate a home for a French diplomat, and you are meeting to discuss ideas. Sergio, with seven years of experience as a designer, believes his is the best decorating plan to follow. Bridgette has only two years of experience, but she studied interior design for one year in France. So far, she has remained quiet during the meeting.

How can you get Bridgette to contribute her ideas?_____

_____

_____

_____

How can you get Sergio to consider ideas other than his own? _____

_____

_____

_____

_____

Impact of Work on Family

Name_____

Date_____ Period _____

Read the case studies below about people who work in the housing industry and answer the questions that follow.

1. Chris is a roofer for a contractor who pays him per job. His pay is based on the size of a roof. Chris quotes a price for his labor and a completion date. His pay is reduced if a job takes longer than promised. Chris is a fast worker, so he makes a good wage on days when he works. Unfortunately, Chris missed over 30 days of work last year due to weather conditions. How might the pressure to work quickly affect Chris personally? _____

_____

How might the way Chris is paid affect his family?_____

_____

2. Lupe and her family live in a rural area in Texas. She has been offered a job as an urban planner in a rapidly growing Chicago suburb. How might life in the Chicago area differ from life in rural Texas for Lupe and her family?

_____

_____

3. Allie recently started her own interior design business. Although Allie enjoys the challenge of being her own boss, she did not realize how difficult it would be to attract clients. She also had not planned on having to meet so many clients on evenings and weekends. How might Allie's lack of clients affect her family?

_____

_____

How might Allie's work schedule affect her family? _____

_____

_____

4. Darnell is a structural engineer who has been working long hours to analyze the design of a large office building. Darnell feels that flaws in the architect's design will impair the building's strength and safety. However, the architect does not seem to respect Darnell's opinion. Darnell is frustrated and angry about the way the architect is treating him. He is also concerned that people could get hurt if the architect does not listen to his advice. How might Darnell's work situation be affecting him personally?

_____

_____

How might Darnell's emotions regarding his work situation affect his family? _____

_____

_____

Balancing Multiple Roles

Activity G

Chapter 27

Name_____

Date_____ Period _____

Interview both members of a dual-career household. Use the symbols below to fill in a weekly schedule for each person, indicating how much time is taken by the activity areas listed. Then, answer the questions that follow.

S Sleep

W Work and commuting to and from a job

H Housework, lawn care, cooking, grocery shopping, helping kids with homework, picking up and dropping off family members, etc.

F Activities involving two or more family members (meals, games, recreational activities, travel, etc.)

P Personal or solitary activities (individual hobbies, reading, watching TV alone, talking with friends, etc.)

Person 1							
Time	Sun.	Mon.	Tues.	Wed.	Thurs.	Fri.	Sat.
1:00 a.m.							
2:00							
3:00							
4:00							
5:00							
6:00							
7.00							
8:00							
9:00							
10:00							
11:00							
12:00 noon							
1:00 p.m.							
2:00							
3:00							
4:00							
5:00							
6:00							
7:00							

(Continued)

Time	Sun.	Mon.	Tues.	Wed.	Thurs.	Fri.	Sat.
8:00							
9:00							
10:00							
11:00							
12:00 midnight							

Person 2							
Time	Sun.	Mon.	Tues.	Wed.	Thurs.	Fri.	Sat.
1:00 a.m.							
2:00							
3:00							
4:00							
5:00							
6:00							
7:00							
8:00							
9:00							
10:00							
11:00							
12:00 noon							
1:00 p.m.							
2:00							
3:00							
4:00							
5:00							
6:00							
7:00							
8:00							
9:00							
10:00							
11:00							
12:00 midnight							

(Continued)

Name_____

Evaluate Results

Calculate approximately how many hours each person spends on each activity area and fill in the chart.

Activity Area	Person 1	Person 2
Sleep		
Work		
Housework		
Family		
Personal		

Does one person spend more time on a particular activity area than the other? Explain._____

_____

_____

_____

_____

_____

_____

_____

What can be done to correct any imbalances within one person's schedule or between household members?

_____

_____

_____

_____

_____

_____

_____

_____

_____

Writing a Resignation Letter

Name_____

Date_____   Period _____

Presume you have worked as a salesperson at a home improvement store called Homebody's for the past three years. There is an economic downturn and fewer customers. Homebody's is laying people off and you fear you will be next. After applying for jobs at other companies, you land a new position. Use the space below to write a letter of resignation to your supervisor giving a two-week notice. Refer to the sample letter of resignation in Figure 27.22 of the text as a guide.

Your name and address

_____

_____

_____

Today's date

_____

Supervisor's Name
Supervisor's Title
Homebody's
555 55th St.
Anytown, Anystate 55555

Dear *Supervisor's Name*:

_____

_____

_____

_____

_____

_____

_____

_____

_____

_____

_____

Sincerely,

_____

Entrepreneurship for Housing and Interiors

Terms for Entrepreneurs

Activity A   Name_____

Chapter 28   Date _____   Period _____

Use the terms below to complete the following sentences by writing the missing word(s) in the space provided to the left of each number.

assets	free market economy	product life cycle
balance sheet	income statement	product trends
business plan	joint venture	profit
chain	labor cost percentage	profit margin
channel of distribution	liabilities	revenues
corporation	loss	shareholder
entrepreneur	market survey	sole proprietorship
equity	partnership	statement of cash flow (SCF)
expenses	physical inventory	target market
franchise		

_____ 1. A person who starts and runs his or her own business is a(n) ____.

_____ 2. The type of business owned by only one person who has full responsibility for the business is known as a(n) ____ ____.

_____ 3. A business owned by two or more owners, usually no more than a small group of people, is called a ____.

_____ 4. A ____ is formed to represent the legal aspects of the business, which is a separate entity from the individual people who own the business.

_____ 5. Individuals who have partial ownership in a company as the result of buying its stock are called ____.

_____ 6. An agreement to sell another company's products or services is called a(n) ____.

_____ 7. A business that has many locations, but whose owner is generally a partnership or corporation, is called a(n) ____.

_____ 8. When an established business joins with one or more companies—sharing the initial investment, profits, and losses—the business option is called a(n) ____ ____.

_____ 9. A ____ ____ is the specific group of people who needs your product or service.

(Continued)

_____ 10. Making sure products are "green," or environmentally safe, is an example of a _____ _____.

_____ 11. Introduction, growth, maturity, and decline are the phases of a _____ _____ _____.

_____ 12. Asking the right questions about client preferences, market price trends, and competing products is part of a(n) _____ _____.

_____ 13. A document that proposes how you will start and run your business is called a(n) _____ _____.

_____ 14. _____ are the cost of doing business.

_____ 15. The money that results from customers purchasing a company's product or service is called *sales*, or _____.

_____ 16. A company makes a _____ when the revenues are greater than expenses.

_____ 17. When a company's expenses are greater than its revenues, the company experiences a(n) _____.

_____ 18. Sometimes referred to as a profit and loss (P&L) statement, _____ _____ is one of three fundamental financial statements used to manage a business.

_____ 19. A second financial statement, or _____ _____, shows what the business owns, its liabilities, and equity on a given date.

_____ 20. Items a company owns that have values, such as cash, physical inventory, buildings, and equipment, are called a company's _____.

_____ 21. Bills payable to suppliers, mortgage loans, or various taxes a business must pay to state or federal governments are its debts or _____.

_____ 22. _____ represents the owner's rights to the assets of the company.

_____ 23. The third fundamental financial statement a business owner uses which shows how cash comes into a business and how it leaves or is used by a business is called a(n) _____ _____ _____ _____.

_____ 24. The route a product takes from the manufacturer to the customer is called the _____ _____ _____.

_____ 25. Visually checking and physically counting the number of items a business has available is known as _____ _____.

_____ 26. A ratio that shows how many dollars in sales a company receives for every dollar spent on wages is called the _____ _____ _____.

_____ 27. Another ratio commonly used to measure a company's profitability by comparing a business' income to its sales is called the _____ _____.

_____ 28. An economic system in which government control is limited and citizens can privately own and operate businesses is called a(n) _____ _____ _____.

Entrepreneurship—Is It for You?

Activity B   Name_____

Chapter 28   Date _____   Period _____

Suppose you are interested in an entrepreneurial career in a housing or interior design profession. Before you start a business, you will need to make many decisions and answer many questions—and those questions and decisions begin with you! Knowing your skills and abilities well—especially with communication—can help guide you on the path to a successful entrepreneurial career. Complete the following chart to help identify your strengths and areas to improve with skills and abilities important to running a business. Then, answer the question that follows the chart.

Skills and Abilities	Strengths	Areas to Improve
Verbal Communication		
Ability to Persuade		
Ability to Negotiate		
Ability to Work Independently		
Creative Ability		
Math/Computer Skills		

Based on your analysis of some skills and abilities essential for entrepreneurship, do you think you would prefer a career as an entrepreneur? Why or why not?

_____

_____

_____

_____

_____

Getting Started—Researching a Business

Name_____

Date_____ Period _____

Presume you want to open your own housing or interior design business; however, you want to make sure there is a solid need for this business in your community before you take this risk. Complete the following to help determine the need for your business. Use the text and the Small Business Administration (SBA) website to help determine your responses.

1. Location of your business: _____

2. Name of your product or service: _____

   _____

3. Your target market (your ideal customers): _____

   _____

4. Who are your competitors? _____

   _____

   A. What products/services do they provide? _____

      _____

   B. What do they charge for their product/services?_____

      _____

5. Conduct market research. What *qualitative* research will you use? What sources of *quantitative* data will you use?

   A. Qualitative:_____

      _____

      _____

   B. Quantitative: _____

      _____

      _____

6. What product trends do you observe in your area that may impact your business?_____

   _____

   _____

7. What demographic trends do you observe in your area that may impact your business? _____

   _____

   _____

8. Based on your preliminary research, do you think your idea for an entrepreneurial business in housing or interior design is a viable option for you in your community? Why or why not?

   _____

   _____

   _____

Business Savvy—Examples and Non-examples

Activity D

Chapter 28

Name_____

Date_____ Period _____

Read through each of the following statements regarding factors that impact business practices. Based on text information, determine if each statement is an *example* or *non-example* of an effective practice for starting a small business. In the space to the left of each statement, write "E" for *example* or "N" for *non-example*.

_____ 1. Demand-based pricing is determined by checking the prices of similar businesses in your area.

_____ 2. Cost-based pricing is determined by calculating how much it costs you to buy or produce an item and then adding a certain percentage to that price for profit.

_____ 3. Competition-based pricing is determined by what customers are prepared to pay for a product or service.

_____ 4. In your business plan, an industry analysis gives details on your product, service, business structure, and how you will run your company.

_____ 5. In your business plan, the marketing strategy describes how you plan to sell your product or service.

_____ 6. A financial plan includes your start-up costs, how much of your own money you will use, who will supply loans, and how you expect to pay back the money.

_____ 7. Before starting a business, you must determine what legal requirements you need to fulfill.

_____ 8. The office of the Secretary of State can inform you of legal restrictions and necessary permits or licenses for operating a business.

_____ 9. Acquiring various types of insurance—including protection from fire or theft, worker's compensation, and business trip insurance—help limit the amount of risk to your business.

_____ 10. A tax identification number is necessary to pay taxes on business profits.

_____ 11. Ongoing operating expenses are the most expensive part of being an entrepreneur because you may need to buy supplies every few months.

_____ 12. Although the cost of support professionals may be expensive, professionals such as an accountant, lawyer, or insurance agent can help limit business risk.

_____ 13. A balance sheet communicates the results of a company's operations for a given period of time such as one month or one year.

_____ 14. A statement of cash flow (SCF) shows how cash comes into a business and how it leaves, or is used by the business.

_____ 15. The goal of a marketing plan is to acquaint customers with the merits of your product or service and persuade them to make purchases.